Project Manager Competency Development (PMCD) Framework

Project Manager Competency Development (PMCD) Framework

Project Management Institute
Newtown Square, Pennsylvania USA

Library of Congress Cataloging-in-Publication Data

Project Management Institute.
    Project manager competency development (PMCD) framework
            p. cm.
        Rev. ed. of: Project manager competency development framework exposure draft. 2001.
        Includes bibliographical references and index.
        ISBN 1-880410-93-1
            1. Project management—Study and teaching. I. Title: Project manager competency
    development framework II. Title: PMCD framwork. III. Project Management Institute.
    IV. Project manager competency development framework exposure draft.

        HD69.P75 P7623 2002
        658.4'04–dc21

                                                            2002028715

ISBN: 1-880410-93-1

Published by: Project Management Institute, Inc.
            Four Campus Boulevard
            Newtown Square, Pennsylvania 19073-3299 USA
            Phone: 610-356-4600 or Visit our website: www.pmi.org
            E-mail: pmihq@pmi.org

Cover design: Rhiannon Thumma
Interior design: Dewey Messer

10   9   8   7   6   5   4   3   2   1

Contents

List of Figures

Foreword

On behalf of the Project Management Institute (PMI®) Board of Directors, I am pleased to present the *Project Manager Competency Development (PMCD) Framework*. PMI has been working to develop standards to support five themes:
- Improve the Performance of Projects
- Improve the Performance of Programs
- Improve the Performance of Project Personnel
- Improve the Performance of Organizations
- Improve the Performance of the Profession.

The *PMCD Framework*, which has been in the works since 1997, is PMI's first standard to address the theme of "Improving the Performance of Project Personnel." This is an important step in PMI's continuing commitment to define the body of knowledge supporting the project management profession, and to develop standards for its application. The *PMCD Framework* is intended to assist project managers and those aspiring to be project managers in guiding their professional development.

The *PMCD Framework* aligns with the *PMBOK® Guide* – 2000 Edition and the *Project Management Professional (PMP®) Role Delineation Study* and current literature. The *PMCD Framework* identifies competencies in three dimensions—Knowledge, Performance and Personal.

Finally, I would like to thank the project team, led by Scott Gill, MBA, PMP – *PMCD Framework* Standard Project Manager and David Violette, MBA, PMP – *PMCD Framework* Standard Deputy Project Manager, who worked so diligently to bring this standard to fruition. Dedicated and competent volunteers have always been the backbone of PMI's success, and this publication is yet another example.

Rebecca Ann Winston, Esq.
2002 Chair – PMI Board of Directors

Preface

This Standard provides guidance on defining project manager competence. The *Project Manager Competency Development (PMCD) Framework* was developed to apply generically to all project managers, regardless of the nature, type, size, or complexity of projects they may be engaged in managing. The targeted audience for this standard includes project managers, those aspiring to be project managers, the organizations that employ both of them, and any associated industry professional groups involved in managing projects. The intent has been to develop a standard to provide individuals and organizations with guidance on how to manage the professional development of the project manager. The PMCD Framework defines the key dimensions of project manager competence and the competencies that are most likely to impact project manager performance as they lead most projects most of the time. While the competencies identified in the PMCD Framework have broad application, the potential differences in the importance placed on particular competencies by organizations within specific industries will need to be considered during the application of the PMCD Framework.

The *Project Manager Competency Development Framework* is consistent with *A Guide to the Project Management Body of Knowledge (PMBOK® Guide)* – 2000 Edition. Additional emphasis was placed on aligning the *PMCD Framework* with the *Project Management Professional (PMP) Role Delineation Study* and the *Project Management Experience and Knowledge Self-Assessment Manual*. The *PMCD Framework* Project team has included information derived from the current literature on project manager competence, competency modeling in general, and other information derived from generally accepted project management sources. The intent of the Project Management Institute (PMI®) Project Management Standards Program is to periodically update the *PMCD Framework*. Your comments are both requested and welcome.

The *PMCD Framework* document is organized as follows:
- Section 1: *Competency Framework Overview*—Provides a working definition of competence and outlines the design and structure of the *PMCD Framework*.
- Section 2: *Project Management Knowledge/Performance Competencies*—Defines the various units of competence, the elements making up each unit, and the performance criteria defining the knowledge and performance dimensions of project manager competence.
- Section 3: *Personal Competencies*—Defines the personal dimension of project manager competence.
- Section 4: *Developing Competence as a Project Manager*—Outlines the recommended methodology for achieving competence as a project manager and includes an example of a Project Manager Competency Summary Scorecard.
- Appendices A–C—Provide background information on the PMI Standards Program and the *PMCD Framework* project.
- Glossary—Provides clarification of key terms used in developing the *PMCD Framework*.
- References—Offers literary support for the information contained in the *PMCD Framework*.
- Index—Gives alphabetical listings and page numbers of key topics covered in the *PMCD Framework*.

both individuals and organiz...

...or the project manager.

Section 1

Competency Framework Overview

Purpose of the *Project Manager Competency Development (PMCD) Framework*

The Project Management Institute (PMI®) sponsored the Project Manager Competency (PMC) project in 1998 to produce a *Framework* for the professional development of project managers. The output of this effort is the *Project Manager Competency Development (PMCD) Framework*. It has been developed to provide both individuals and organizations with guidance on how to manage the professional development of the project manager.

The *PMCD Framework* is based on the premise that competencies have a direct effect on performance. The degree or extent of this impact may vary, depending on certain factors such as project types and characteristics, or organizational context. Although the *PMCD Framework* recognizes these factors, at this point in the development of the standard, it does not attempt to address them directly. The *PMCD Framework* defines the key dimensions of project manager competence and the competencies that are most likely to impact project manager performance. Therefore, while the competencies identified by the *PMCD Framework* have a broad application, the potential differences in the importance of particular competencies, given certain organizational contexts or project types or characteristics, still need to be considered during the application of the *PMCD Framework*.

The *PMCD Framework* draws heavily on *A Guide to the Project Management Body of Knowledge (PMBOK® Guide) – 2000 Edition*, as well as the *Project Management Experience and Knowledge Self-Assessment Manual* and the *Project Management Professional (PMP) Role Delineation Study*. Although the *PMCD Framework* is aligned with these sources, it has its own perspective in that it has neither a pure process group nor knowledge area focus. By identifying the applicable performance criteria by knowledge area and process group, it helps describe the necessary knowledge, performance, and behavior for a competent project manager.

What Is Competence?

In Lynn Crawford's work on determining global project management competencies, *A Global Approach to Project Management Competence* (1997), she states:

> Competence is a term which is widely used but which has come to mean different things to different people. It is generally accepted, however, as encompassing knowledge, skills, attitudes and behaviors that are causally related to superior job performance (Boyatzis 1982). This understanding of competence has been described as *attribute-based inference of competence* (Heywood, Gonczi, et al. 1992). To

this can be added what is referred to as the *performance-based* approach to competence, which assumes that competence can be inferred from demonstrated performance at pre-defined acceptable standards in the workplace (Gonczi, Hager, et al. 1993). The performance-based approach is the basis for what has become known as the Competency Standards Movement that underpins the National Vocation Qualifications in the United Kingdom, the Australian National Competency Standards Framework [linked to the Australian Qualifications Framework] and the National Qualifications Framework of the New Zealand Qualifications Authority (NZQA).

The concepts contained within this description formed the basis of the *PMCD Framework*.

A Working Definition

The PMC Project incorporates the components of competence shown here into the working definition of competence for the development of the *PMCD Framework*.

> Based on Scott Parry's (1998) definition, a **competency** is a cluster of related knowledge, attitudes, skills, and other personal characteristics that:
> - Affects a major part of one's job (i.e., one or more key roles or responsibilities)
> - Correlates with performance on the job
> - Can be measured against well-accepted standards
> - Can be improved via training and development
> - Can be broken down into dimensions of competence.

When applied to project management, competence can be described as consisting of three separate dimensions (Crawford 1997):

1. What individual project managers bring to a project or project-related activity through their knowledge and understanding of project management. This dimension is called ***Project Management Knowledge*** *(i.e., what they know about project management)*

and

2. What individual project managers are able to demonstrate in their ability to successfully manage the project or complete project-related activities. This dimension is called ***Project Management Performance*** *(i.e., what they are able to do or accomplish while applying their project management knowledge)*

in combination with

3. The core personality characteristics underlying a person's capability to do a project or project activity (Finn 1993; Crawford 1997). This dimension is called ***Personal Competency*** *(i.e., how individuals behave when performing the project or activity; their attitudes and core personality traits)*.

It is generally accepted that, to be recognized as fully competent, an individual would need to be evaluated successfully against each of these dimensions. It would be impossible for project managers to be judged competent if they did not possess the "right" combination of *knowledge*, *performance*, and *personal* competence.

This *PMCD Framework* is illustrated in Figure 1-1. It shows how the three dimensions of competence come together to help the project manager accomplish the level of project performance desired by the organization.

Project Manager Competency and Project Success

An important note is that a "competent" project manager alone does not guarantee project success. PMI believes that project success requires project manager competence, as well as organizational project management maturity and capability—organizational performance cannot be ignored. In other words, having a project manager who possesses the "right" competencies cannot ensure project success.

Dimensions of Competency

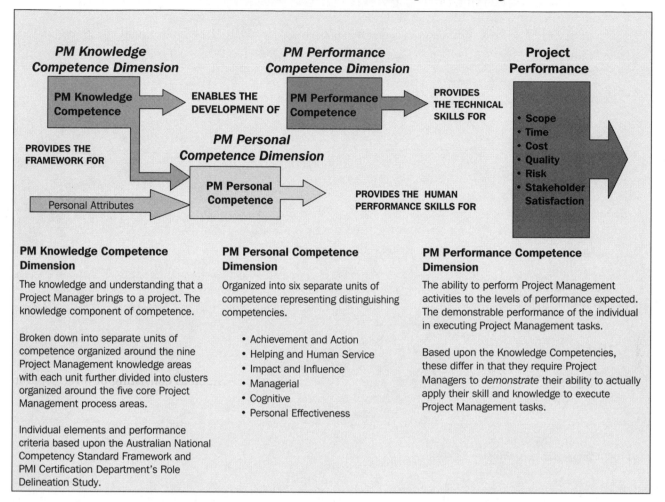

Figure 1-1. Dimensions of Competency

Focusing solely on project manager competence, regardless of the organization's performance, is too simplistic. There are too many organizational maturity factors and other contingencies that influence the outcome of the project as well. In fact, it is possible to have a "competent" project manager working within an "immature" organization, which could result in an unsuccessful project, or vice versa.

This concept is illustrated in Figure 1-2. It shows how project manager competency and organizational maturity are required to consistently obtain project success, and how both of these can be influenced by various contingency or moderating variables. The figure, along with the definitions of project performance (in the next paragraph) and project success (in the subsequent paragraph), are based on work performed by PMI Standards Program teams for the *PMCD Framework* and the Organizational Project Management Maturity Model (OPM3), as captured in the summary of Phase 2 work by the Initial PMCD Framework Project Team.

The *Components of Project Success* illustration shows how the competency of the project manager provides the basis for overall project performance. Project performance is defined as *the extent to which the project is carried out as planned in terms of objectives, time and financial constraints, and organizational policy and procedures.* This definition places more emphasis on the process of how the project was carried out. It is the project manager's role to lead the project through these processes.

Project performance is shown as having a major impact upon overall project success. After all, if the project does not follow the specified plans or processes, it will be difficult to obtain ultimate success

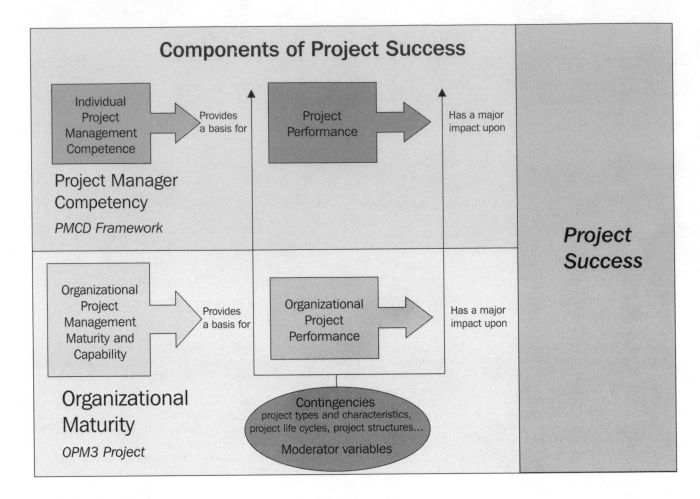

Figure 1-2. Components of Project Success

with the project. Success of the project looks at what was achieved by the project. Perception of project success can vary, depending upon the perspective of the various stakeholders. There is the perspective of the client or customer—how does that individual view the project's achievements? There are also the perspectives of the other stakeholders to consider—those of the project manager, project team members, project sponsor, performing organization, and other stakeholders. It is the collective agreement of these stakeholders, regarding the degree to which the project has met its objectives, that truly defines whether the project is viewed as a success.

As the *PMCD Framework* clearly shows, even when there is a competent project manager leading the efforts toward strong project performance, the influences of the performing organization, as well as other contingency variables, can affect overall project success. Thus, project manager competence by itself cannot guarantee project success.

It is not the intent of the *PMCD Framework* to address these other factors in project success. Rather, it looks solely at the competencies needed to help project managers be successful in their role. Performing organizations will always need to evaluate the "right" mix of competencies required of their project managers.

Project Management Competence and Specific Application Competence

As the *PMCD Framework* is based upon the principles and processes of the *PMBOK® Guide*, it describes the generic competencies needed in most projects, in most organizations, and in most industries. There are, however, a number of areas that the *PMCD Framework* does not address. In some industries, there may be technical skills that are particularly relevant to that industry or that may be covered by specific legislation.

For example, an organization primarily involved in conducting information technology projects may require that its project managers possess a specific competency level around information technology, as well as competence in project management. The *PMCD Framework* does not address application-specific competence. The intent of the *PMCD Framework* is to provide the generic foundations for project manager competence. Individual project managers, or their organizations, may choose to supplement these generic competencies with additional application-specific competencies to meet their specific needs.

Design and Structure of the PMCD Framework

Design of the *PMCD Framework*

The *PMCD Framework* has been designed and developed to incorporate the three dimensions of competence. The intent is to ensure that the individuals themselves, their organizations, and associated industry professional bodies apply a rigorous methodology for the development, assessment, and recognition of competence in individual project managers.

The *PMCD Framework* has been designed to:
• Be simple to understand and straightforward to use
• Cover the range of competencies that a project manager needs to do the job.

The *PMCD Framework* has also been developed to apply generically to all project managers, regardless of the nature, type, size, or complexity of projects in which they are engaged—in other words, to apply to project managers leading most projects most of the time. The generic nature of the *PMCD Framework* is necessary to ensure that:
• Project management competence in individuals is transferable across industries
• Industries and organizations are able to utilize the *PMCD Framework* as a basis for the development of more industry- and organization-specific competency models.

The *PMCD Framework* has drawn upon:
• Input from organizations and industries on an international basis
• The framework developed for the *PMBOK® Guide* by the Project Management Institute (PMI)
• PMI Certification Department's *Project Management Experience and Knowledge Self-Assessment Manual* and *Project Management Professional (PMP) Role Delineation Study*
• The competency framework contained in the National Competency Standards for Project Management, endorsed by the Australian Institute of Project Management (AIPM)
• The behavioral competencies identified and documented in the competency dictionary developed by Lyle and Signe Spencer (1993) and adapted for use in the *PMCD Framework*.

Structure of the Overall *PMCD Framework*

The Project Management (PM) Knowledge and Performance Competence dimensions draw upon the nine knowledge areas of project management, as well as the five project management process groups, as outlined in the *PMBOK® Guide*. The *PMCD Framework* has also been designed to outline the PM Personal Competence dimension. Thus, by outlining the three dimensions of competence, the *PMCD Framework* provides an overall view of knowledge, skills, and behaviors one would have to develop to build competence as a project manager.

The *PMCD Framework* document is divided into four sections:
• Section 1: *Competency Framework Overview*—This Overview section introduces the discussion of project manager competence.
• Section 2: *Project Management Knowledge/Performance Competencies*—This section provides a detailed description of the Project Management Knowledge Competencies identified as applying to project managers leading most projects most of the time. Since Project Management Performance Competencies are the demonstrable performance of project managers executing what they know, the Project Management Performance Competencies are also included in this section.

- Section 3: *Personal Competencies*—This section provides the details of the personal dimension of project manager competence.
- Section 4: *Developing Competence as a Project Manager*—This section outlines a suggested five-step methodology for developing competence as a project manager. This section also provides an example of a simple assessment summary tool that could be used, either by an individual project manager or by the manager's organization, to assess overall strengths in the competencies outlined in the *PMCD Framework*.

Structure of the Project Management Knowledge and Performance Competencies

*The following components, illustrated in Tables 1-1 through 1-3, pertain to **all** the tables in Section 2.*

The Project Management Knowledge and Performance Competencies provided in the *PMCD Framework* are structured as follows:

1. **Units of Competence.** Units of Competence describe, in broad terms, what is expected of project management personnel in particular aspects of the job. A Unit is able to stand alone as a complete function in the area of employment. Each Unit of Competence in this section of the *PMCD Framework* corresponds to a Knowledge Area of project management.

2. **Competency Clusters.** Competency Clusters are included in the structure of the *PMCD Framework*, and correspond to the project management process groups of Initiating, Planning, Executing, Controlling, and Closing.

3. **Elements.** Each Unit of Competence and Competency Cluster consists of a number of Elements, which reflect the competencies that project managers are expected to possess.

4. **Performance Criteria.** Each Element is described by Performance Criteria, which specify the outcomes to be achieved in order to demonstrate competent performance. Performance Criteria form the basis upon which evidence of competence can be assessed.

5. **Examples of Assessment Guidelines.** The Project Management Knowledge/Performance Competencies section of the *PMCD Framework* includes Examples of Assessment Guidelines, which outline the requirements for evaluation and/or assessment of competence in each particular Unit of Competence. Separate guidelines are provided for assessing the Knowledge Competencies and the Performance Competencies.

The Units of Competence, Competency Clusters, Elements, and Performance Criteria, contained within the Project Management Knowledge/Performance Competencies, are organized in the following type of hierarchy. (An explanation of the numbering scheme and symbols follows.)

__.# Unit of Competence
    __.#.# COMPETENCY CLUSTER
        __.#.#.# Element (specific to each Competency Cluster)
            _.#.#.#.# Performance Criterion (specific to each Element)

Note: The first character (represented by an underscore) can be a "K" or a "P", depending on the interpretation of the performance criterion.

This hierarchy is repeated for each Unit of Competence and COMPETENCY CLUSTER. However, each combination bears a unique numbering sequence, as represented by the pound signs (#).

An example of the tabular format is shown in Table 1-3. This format is used for each of the different Units of Competence within the Project Management Knowledge and Project Management Performance Competencies. (Note: The table is only an example; the complete listing of Knowledge and Performance Competencies is contained in Section 2 of the *PMCD Framework*.)

Numbering Scheme for Project Management Knowledge and Performance Competencies

Tables 1-1 and 1-2 outline the numbering scheme used for the Project Management Knowledge and Performance Competencies.

A numbering scheme has been established to help the reader locate particular performance criteria related to the Knowledge and Performance Competencies. This numbering scheme can also help the

Unit of Competence and Number①	Competency Cluster②	Cluster Number②		Element Number③	Performance Criterion Number④
_.1 Project Integration Management	Initiating	Knowledge	K.1.1	K.1.1.1	K.1.1.1.1
		Performance	P.1.1	P.1.1.1	P.1.1.1.1
_.2 Project Scope Management	Initiating	Knowledge	K.2.1	K.2.1.1	K.2.1.1.1
		Performance	P.2.1	P.2.1.1	P.2.1.1.1
_.3 Project Time Management	Initiating	Knowledge	K.3.1	K.3.1.1	K.3.1.1.1
		Performance	P.3.1	P.3.1.1	P.3.1.1.1
_.4 Project Cost Management	Initiating	Knowledge	K.4.1	K.4.1.1	K.4.1.1.1
		Performance	P.4.1	P.4.1.1	P.4.1.1.1
_.5 Project Quality Management	Initiating	Knowledge	K.5.1	K.5.1.1	K.5.1.1.1
		Performance	P.5.1	P.5.1.1	P.5.1.1.1
_.6 Project Human Resources Management	Initiating	Knowledge	K.6.1	K.6.1.1	K.6.1.1.1
		Performance	P.6.1	P.6.1.1	P.6.1.1.1
_.7 Project Communications Management	Initiating	Knowledge	K.7.1	K.7.1.1	K.7.1.1.1
		Performance	P.7.1	P.7.1.1	P.7.1.1.1
_.8 Project Risk Management	Initiating	Knowledge	K.8.1	K.8.1.1	K.8.1.1.1
		Performance	P.8.1	P.8.1.1	P.8.1.1.1
_.9 Project Procurement Management	Initiating	Knowledge	K.9.1	K.9.1.1	K.9.1.1.1
		Performance	P.9.1	P.9.1.1	P.9.1.1.1

① The underscore represents either a "K" (for Knowledge) or a "P" (for Performance)

② This table utilizes the Initiating competency cluster, and its associated numbering, as an example. The other four competency clusters (Planning, Executing, Controlling, Closing) each bear a different number, as shown in Table 1-2

③ For exemplary purposes only; the last digit may vary

④ For exemplary purposes only; the last two digits may vary

Table 1-1. Numbering scheme of the Project Management Knowledge and Performance Competencies

reader understand the relationship between specific performance criteria in the *PMCD Framework* and the elements, clusters, and units of competence.

The first character in the sequence identifies whether a performance criterion is being viewed either from a Project Management **Knowledge** Competency perspective or from a Project Management **Performance** Competency perspective. If it is being viewed from a Knowledge Competency perspective, it is assigned a "K" as the first character in its criterion number. Conversely, a Performance Competency criterion is assigned a "P" as the first character in its criterion number.

The fact that the units, clusters, elements, and performance criteria outlined in these two dimensions of competence are the same makes this numbering distinction necessary. Though the criteria appear to be the same, they are distinct from each other strictly on the basis of from which perspective they are being viewed—either from a knowledge perspective or from a performance perspective. Thus, performance criterion K.3.2.3.2 (*Utilize simulations* as part of the element *Conduct Activity Duration Estimating* within the *Planning* cluster of the *Project Time Management* unit of competence) is being viewed from the perspective of the project manager's knowledge of the use of simulations to conduct activity duration estimates. If the criterion had been identified as P.3.2.3.2, then the perspective would be whether the project manager could actually produce activity duration estimates using simulation techniques such as Monte Carlo analysis.

Structure of the Project Management Personal Competencies

The same basic structure is used to outline the Personal Competencies. Separate Clusters represent Personal Competencies in the *PMCD Framework*. These are based on the Competency Dictionary developed by Lyle and Signe Spencer and published in their book *Competence at Work* (1993). The PMC project team modified the competency descriptors contained in the Competency Dictionary to be reflective of

Unit of Competence	Competency Cluster									
	Initiating		Planning		Executing		Controlling		Closing	
	Know	Perform	Know	Perform	Know	Perform	Know	Perform	Know	Perform
Project Integration Management	K.1.1	P.1.1	K.1.2	P.1.2	K.1.3	P.1.3	K.1.4	P.1.4	K.1.5	P.1.5
Project Scope Management	K.2.1	P.2.1	K.2.2	P.2.2	K.2.3	P.2.3	K.2.4	P.2.4	K.2.5	P.2.5
Project Time Management	K.3.1	P.3.1	K.3.2	P.3.2	K.3.3	P.3.3	K.3.4	P.3.4	K.3.5	P.3.5
Project Cost Management	K.4.1	P.4.1	K.4.2	P.4.2	K.4.3	P.4.3	K.4.4	P.4.4	K.4.5	P.4.5
Project Quality Management	K.5.1	P.5.1	K.5.2	P.5.2	K.5.3	P.5.3	K.5.4	P.5.4	K.5.5	P.5.5
Project Human Resources Management	K.6.1	P.6.1	K.6.2	P.6.2	K.6.3	P.6.3	K.6.4	P.6.4	K.6.5	P.6.5
Project Communications Management	K.7.1	P.7.1	K.7.2	P.7.2	K.7.3	P.7.3	K.7.4	P.7.4	K.7.5	P.7.5
Project Risk Management	K.8.1	P.8.1	K.8.2	P.8.2	K.8.3	P.8.3	K.8.4	P.8.4	K.8.5	P.8.5
Project Procurement Management	K.9.1	P.9.1	K.9.2	P.9.2	K.9.3	P.9.3	K.9.4	P.9.4	K.9.5	P.9.5

Table 1-2. Numbering scheme of the Project Management Knowledge and Performance Units of Competency ("K" represents Knowledge; "P" represents Performance)

project manager personal competence. These Competency Clusters are grouped in six separate Units of Competence. Each Unit contains from two to four Clusters of related behavioral descriptors.

Each Cluster is further broken down into one or more Elements reflecting the level of autonomy, drive, or urgency displayed relating to the competency. Performance Criteria are then provided to describe the behavior expected around the Elements.

Examples of Assessment Guidelines are not provided for Personal Competencies. Rather, evaluation is performed by assessing whether the project manager exhibits the behaviors reflected in the performance criteria listed in this section of the *PMCD Framework*.

The Units of Competence and Clusters contained within the Personal Competencies are as follows:

Unit of Competence: Achievement and Action
- Achievement Orientation Cluster
- Concern for Order, Quality, and Accuracy Cluster
- Initiative Cluster
- Information Seeking Cluster

Unit of Competence: Helping and Human Service
- Customer Service Orientation Cluster
- Interpersonal Understanding Cluster

Unit of Competence: Impact and Influence
- Impact and Influence Cluster
- Organizational Awareness Cluster
- Relationship Building Cluster

Unit of Competence: Managerial
- Teamwork and Cooperation Cluster
- Developing Others Cluster
- Team Leadership Cluster
- Directiveness: Assertiveness and Use of Positional Power Cluster

_.1 Unit of Competence—Project Integration Management	
_.1.1 COMPETENCY CLUSTER: Initiating	
Elements	**Performance Criteria**
_.1.1.1 **Identify and Document Project Needs Developing Project-Related Product or Service Descriptions**	.1 Determine product/service characteristics using expert judgment as needed. .2 Identify/document constraints and assumptions.
_.1.1.2 **Perform an Initial Project Feasibility Study and Analysis**	.1 Utilize project selection methods/decision models, including benefit measurement methods and constrained optimization methods. .2 Evaluate historical information for projects involving similar products and services. .3 Perform high-level assessment of the organizational resources for the project. .4 Perform high-level assessment of the technical and non-technical requirements of the project.
Examples of Assessment Guidelines	

KNOWLEDGE COMPETENCIES

Demonstrate a knowledge and understanding of:

- The inputs to project initiation.

- The tools and techniques utilized for initiating and appraising projects.

- The outputs of project initiation.

PERFORMANCE COMPETENCIES

Demonstrate an ability to perform a:

- Needs Requirement.

- Feasibility Study/Statement.

Table 1-3. Example of the Knowledge and Performance Competencies tabular format

Unit of Competence: Cognitive
- Analytical Thinking Cluster
- Conceptual Thinking Cluster

Unit of Competence: Personal Effectiveness
- Self-Control Cluster
- Self-Confidence Cluster
- Flexibility Cluster
- Organizational Commitment Cluster

These Units of Competence were chosen to represent those personal and behavioral competencies considered to be important to a competent project manager.

Numbering Scheme for Project Management Personal Competencies

The Personal Competencies use a similar numbering scheme to identify the specific performance criteria within the *Framework*. Table 1-4 outlines the numbering scheme used for the Project Management Personal Competencies. This dimension of competence uses a "B" as the first character in the criterion number. The numbering scheme further breaks down the details of this dimension of competence by outlining the various levels of units, clusters, elements, and performance criteria. Thus, just as with

Unit of Competence and Number	Competency Cluster	Cluster Number	Element Number[1]	Performance Criterion Number[2]
B.1 Achievement and Action	Achievement Orientation	B.1.1	B.1.1.1	B.1.1.1.1
	Concern for Order, Quality, and Accuracy	B.1.2	B.1.2.1	B.1.2.1.1
	Initiative	B.1.3	B.1.3.1	B.1.3.1.1
	Information Seeking	B.1.4	B.1.4.1	B.1.4.1.1
B.2 Helping and Human Service	Customer Service Orientation	B.2.1	B.2.1.1	B.2.1.1.1
	Interpersonal Understanding	B.2.2	B.2.2.1	B.2.2.1.1
B.3 Impact and Influence	Impact and Influence	B.3.1	B.3.1.1	B.3.1.1.1
	Organizational Awareness	B.3.2	B.3.2.1	B.3.2.1.1
	Relationship Building	B.3.3	B.3.3.1	B.3.3.1.1
B.4 Managerial	Teamwork and Cooperation	B.4.1	B.4.1.1	B.4.1.1.1
	Developing Others	B.4.2	B.4.2.1	B.4.2.1.1
	Team Leadership	B.4.3	B.4.3.1	B.4.3.1.1
	Directiveness: Assertiveness and Use of Positional Power	B.4.4	B.4.4.1	B.4.4.1.1
B.5 Cognitive	Analytical Thinking	B.5.1	B.5.1.1	B.5.1.1.1
	Conceptual Thinking	B.5.2	B.5.2.1	B.5.2.1.1
B.6 Personal Effectiveness	Self-Control	B.6.1	B.6.1.1	B.6.1.1.1
	Self-Confidence	B.6.2	B.6.2.1	B.6.2.1.1
	Flexibility	B.6.3	B.6.3.1	B.6.3.1.1
	Organizational Commitment	B.6.4	B.6.4.1	B.6.4.1.1

[1] For exemplary purposes only; the last digit may vary

[2] For exemplary purposes only; the last two digits may vary

Table 1-4. Numbering scheme of the Project Management Personal Competencies ("B" represents Behavior)

the other dimensions of competence, the numbering scheme allows the reader to see the relationship between individual criteria, elements, and clusters.

Each Unit of Competence and its associated Clusters in the Personal Competency section of the *PMCD Framework* follows a standard format, as shown in Table 1-5. (Note: Table 1-5 is only an example; the complete listing of Personal Competencies is contained in Section 3 of the *PMCD Framework*.)

A Graphical View of the Overall PMCD Framework Structure

A graphical view of the *PMCD Framework* is provided in Figure 1-3 to aid the reader in visualizing how the different components and dimensions build on each other to develop the overall competency of the project manager.

Using the PMCD Framework

What the *PMCD Framework* Provides

Before starting to use the *PMCD Framework* in the workplace—either as a practitioner, an employer, or an advisor—the *PMCD Framework* and Guidelines **should be read and understood**. It is important to

B.1 Unit of Competence—Achievement and Action	
B.1.1 COMPETENCY CLUSTER: Achievement Orientation Achievement Orientation is a concern for working well, or for competing against, a standard of excellence.	
Element	**Performance Criteria**
B.1.1.1 Operates with Intensity to Achieve Project Goals	.1 Focuses on task(s) and standards of excellence set by relevant project stakeholders. .2 Strives to do job well, reaching goals set by project stakeholders. .3 Controls project risk proactively. .4 Sets high performance standards for self-acting as a role model for team.
B.1.1.2 Motivates Project Stakeholders in a Positive Way	.1 Strives to ensure that expectations of all stakeholders are achieved. .2 Drives increased effectiveness of the project team and the way it does business.
B.1.1.3 Provides New Solutions in Planning and Delivering Projects	.1 Performs innovative actions to improve performance of the project team.
B.1.1.4 Operates with Individual Integrity and Personal Professionalism	.1 Adheres to all legal requirements. .2 Works within a recognized set of ethical standards. .3 Discloses to all stakeholders any possible conflict of interest. .4 Neither offers nor accepts inappropriate payments or any other items for personal gain. .5 Maintains and respects confidentiality of sensitive information.

Table 1-5. Example of the Personal Competencies tabular format

become comfortable with the content of the *PMCD Framework* and what it indicates in regard to competency as a project manager. The *PMCD Framework* provides a summary of the competencies viewed as supporting success as a project manager.

The perspective of the *PMCD Framework* looks at the project manager's role through a combined process group and knowledge area matrix, identifying the performance criteria relative to a knowledge area for each process group. An additional dimension for personal competence looks at the project manager behavior relative to overall competence in managing projects.

For an **employer**, the *PMCD Framework* gives a "framework" of the skills, knowledge, understanding, and behavior required by project managers, in order to fulfill their project manager role within the organization. By using the *PMCD Framework*, one can discover the existing skills of the work force, as well as any gaps that may exist and may require additional training or education.

For a **project manager practitioner** or as a **member of a project team**, the *PMCD Framework* helps identify the areas in which one is already competent (and can prove it), and those where further development or experience is needed.

For an **advisor** to an organization, the *PMCD Framework* provides a powerful tool to help scan and analyze the existing skills within the organization and to discover any gaps that may need to be addressed.

Tailoring the *Project Manager Competency Development Framework*

The units, clusters, and elements of the *PMCD Framework* are intended to represent the ideal project manager. It has been designed to be generally acceptable, applying to most projects most of the time. Therefore, organizations must use their own discretion when customizing the relevant elements of the *PMCD Framework* to apply to their way of doing business. In other words, the *PMCD Framework* should be tailored to represent the organization's view of a project manager. An organization may choose to tailor the Framework to not only select the competencies relevant to their line of business or organization, but they may also choose to specify the relative importance of different competencies, or the

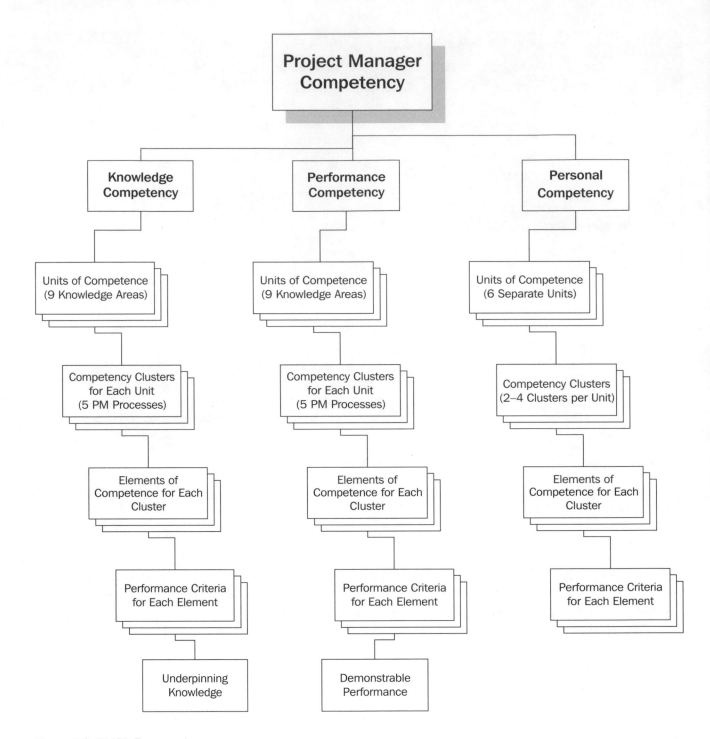

Figure 1-3. PMCD Framework

required level of mastery for each competency. The five-step process outlined in Section 4—*Developing Competence as a Project Manager* lays out a methodology for accomplishing this.

However, organizations must realize that the *PMCD Framework* is based on a project manager being competent to lead most projects most of the time. The more an organization deviates from the *PMCD Framework* by scaling back its model, by deselecting elements and the respective performance criteria, or diminishing the relative importance of various criteria contained in the *PMCD Framework*, the more the organization risks the project manager's competency to practice in other industries and environments. To maximize transportability between industries and environments, an organization is strongly encouraged to keep as much as is feasible of the *PMCD Framework* intact within its business environment.

Section 2

Project Management Knowledge/ Performance Competencies

Both Project Management Knowledge and Project Management Performance Competencies are assessable—i.e., they can be objectively measured and quantified in individuals. However, for this to occur, endorsed standards or benchmarks are required against which:

individuals are able to record and plan their progress toward competence, and/or

organizations are able to design and develop performance measurement instruments, training and education programs, and employment specifications.

The *PMCD Framework* provides a standard recommended through the collective opinion of the project management community who provided input into its development. The *PMCD Framework* can help organizations or individuals design their own approaches to perform accurate assessment and, subsequently, the necessary design mechanism for organizations to develop these instruments, programs, and specifications. It provides the foundation for a methodology to achieve competence (see Section 4), which can be applied by both individuals and organizations.

Purpose of the Project Management Knowledge and Performance Competencies

The **Project Management Knowledge/Performance Competencies,** outlined in this section of the *PMCD Framework,* provide a basis for guidance to develop the instruments required for assessing these competencies. In order to be judged fully competent, as defined by the units of competence outlined in these two dimensions of the *PMCD Framework*, a project manager would have to be viewed as satisfying the performance criteria defining the individual elements of competence. Organizations would have to determine the overall relevance of the discrete elements and performance criteria when constructing their assessment instruments. However, it should be kept in mind that the *PMCD Framework* was developed to describe competence in project managers needed in leading most projects most of the time. The generic nature of the *PMCD Framework* was constructed to ensure that project manager competence in individuals would be transferable across organizations and industries.

It is envisioned that both individuals and organizations will be able to use this part of the *PMCD Framework* as a basis for professional development. Mechanisms for the assessment of individuals in these dimensions could include knowledge tests, such as the Project Management Professional (PMP®)

exam for testing Project Management Knowledge Competence, or a review of the actual work products produced by the project manager as a means of evaluating Project Management Performance Competence. Assessment mechanisms could also include instruments such as a full 360-degree Feedback process, as well as individual Peer and/or Self-Reviews, to help determine the level of project manager competence in these dimensions.

As previously described in Section 1, the various Units of Competence can be represented in tabular format. On the following pages, Tables 2-1 through 2-45 utilize such a format, wherein each pertains to a different Unit of Competence, along with their associated Competency Clusters. Each of the Competency Clusters is further broken down into pertinent Elements and Performance Criteria. Note that each table also utilizes the numbering scheme originally detailed in Section 1.

Unit of Competence—Project Integration Management

_.1 Unit of Competence—Project Integration Management	
_.1.1 COMPETENCY CLUSTER: Initiating	
Elements	**Performance Criteria**
_.1.1.1 Identify and Document Project Needs Developing Project-Related Product or Service Descriptions	.1 Determine product/service characteristics using expert judgment as needed. .2 Identify/document constraints and assumptions.
_.1.1.2 Perform an Initial Project Feasibility Study and Analysis	.1 Utilize project selection methods/decision models, including benefit measurement methods and constrained optimization methods. .2 Evaluate historical information for projects involving similar products and services. .3 Perform high-level assessment of the organizational resources for the project. .4 Perform high-level assessment of the technical and non-technical requirements of the project.
Examples of Assessment Guidelines	

KNOWLEDGE COMPETENCIES

Demonstrate a knowledge and understanding of:

- The inputs to project initiation.
- The tools and techniques utilized for initiating and appraising projects.
- The outputs of project initiation.

PERFORMANCE COMPETENCIES

Demonstrate an ability to develop a:

- Needs Requirement.
- Project Feasibility Study/Statement.

Table 2-1. Project Integration Management: Initiating

_.1 Unit of Competence—Project Integration Management	
_.1.2 COMPETENCY CLUSTER: Planning	
Elements	**Performance Criteria**
_.1.2.1 Conduct Project Plan Development (*PMBOK® Guide* 4.1)	.1 Determine the project plan development methodology. .2 Identify the project stakeholders and project/organization responsibility relationships. .3 Identify the interface points with other projects within the organization. .4 Develop a stakeholder management plan. .5 Define and utilize a Project Management Information System to assist in the gathering, integration, interpretation, and dissemination of the inputs and outputs of all project processes. .6 Identify and develop an integrated project plan, including the project charter, the scope statement, the Work Breakdown Structure (WBS), responsibility assignments, schedules, milestones, key staffing requirements, budgets, performance measurement baselines, lists of key risks, risk response plans, management review plans outlining the project management approach, the project execution plan, and other subsidiary management plans. .7 Determine the overall project management plan for use in managing and controlling project execution. .8 Describe the difference between dynamically updating the project plan and preserving the project performance measurement baseline (Knowledge only).
Examples of Assessment Guidelines	

KNOWLEDGE COMPETENCIES

Demonstrate a knowledge and understanding of:

- The inputs to project plan development.
- The tools and techniques utilized for the development of the project plan.
- The outputs of project plan development.

PERFORMANCE COMPETENCIES

Demonstrate an ability to develop:

- Project Plan.
- Project Management Plan.
- Stakeholder Management Plan.

Table 2-2. Project Integration Management: Planning

_.1 Unit of Competence—Project Integration Management	
_.1.3 COMPETENCY CLUSTER: Executing	
Elements	**Performance Criteria**
_.1.3.1 Conduct Project Plan Execution (*PMBOK® Guide* 4.2)	.1 Identify and execute preventive actions or modifications to the project plan using a structured approach. .2 Utilize structured communication methods. .3 Utilize regularly scheduled project status reviews. .4 Utilize project information systems to provide project information. .5 Utilize negotiating strategies. .6 Apply problem-solving techniques in managing the project. .7 Implement methods used to influence behavior and preventive action. .8 Manage various project-related technical and/or organizational interfaces. .9 Utilize work authorization systems and procedures for approving project work to ensure proper work sequencing. .10 Know products and services, and have ability to monitor/react to project changes initiated by the sponsor. .11 Document work results and quality outcomes, including completion of project deliverables. .12 Identify change requests during work processes, and determine potential project scope changes.
Examples of Assessment Guidelines	

KNOWLEDGE COMPETENCIES

Demonstrate a knowledge and understanding of:
- The inputs to project plan execution.
- The tools and techniques utilized for executing the project plan.
- The outputs of project plan execution.

PERFORMANCE COMPETENCIES

Demonstrate an ability to produce:
- Change Requests.
- Work Results.

Table 2-3. Project Integration Management: Executing

_.1 Unit of Competence—Project Integration Management	
_.1.4 COMPETENCY CLUSTER: Controlling	
Elements	**Performance Criteria**
_.1.4.1 **Conduct Integrated Change Control** (*PMBOK® Guide* 4.3)	.1 Verify that a change has occurred. .2 Determine that a change is needed and that change request documentation has been properly completed. .3 Adhere to the steps by which official project documents may be changed. .4 Determine whether variances from the plan require corrective action, need new or revised cost estimates, should result in a modification of activity sequences, or require the development of additional risk response alternatives. .5 Utilize the powers and responsibilities of the change control board or other governing body. .6 Document and implement procedures to process changes that may be accepted without prior change control board review or other governing body. .7 Employ proactive, structured change management procedures to properly influence a variety of project stakeholders. .8 Utilize the performing organization's change control system. .9 Complete project plan modifications, including integration with various project baselines. .10 Utilize configuration management procedures to integrate change across all areas of the project.
Examples of Assessment Guidelines	

KNOWLEDGE COMPETENCIES

Demonstrate a knowledge and understanding of:

- The inputs to integrated change control.
- The tools and techniques utilized for conducting integrated change control.
- The outputs of integrated change control.

PERFORMANCE COMPETENCIES

Demonstrate an ability to develop:

- Project Plan Updates.
- Performance Reports.

Table 2-4. Project Integration Management: Controlling

_.1 Unit of Competence—Project Integration Management	
_.1.5 COMPETENCY CLUSTER: Closing	
Elements	**Performance Criteria**
_.1.5.1 **Conduct Project Closure with Regard to Integration**	.1 Document lessons learned from project integration, including causes of activities requiring corrective action, types of activities requiring corrective action, reasons for selecting certain corrective actions, and classification of changes for subsequent analysis.
Examples of Assessment Guidelines	

KNOWLEDGE COMPETENCIES

Demonstrate a knowledge and understanding of:

- The inputs to project closure with regard to project integration processes.
- The tools and techniques utilized for project closure.
- The outputs of project closure with regard to project integration processes.

PERFORMANCE COMPETENCIES

Demonstrate an ability to develop:

- Lessons Learned.

Table 2-5. Project Integration Management: Closing

Unit of Competence—Project Scope Management

_.2 Unit of Competence—Project Scope Management	
_.2.1 COMPETENCY CLUSTER: Initiating	
Elements	**Performance Criteria**
_.2.1.1 Prepare Project Charter (*PMBOK® Guide* 5.1)	.1 Develop a project charter to formally document and link the project to the ongoing work of the organization. .2 Define the responsibilities of the project manager and other organizational managers. .3 Identify how project budget concerns and resource availability affect the project, and how to interface with the project sponsor or other organizational managers with resource responsibility. .4 Define project phases of the project life cycle. .5 Develop the primary components of the project charter. .6 Identify project stakeholders. .7 Establish project purpose, description, assumptions, and constraints. .8 Define project business benefits and benefit measurements. .9 Define critical success factors.

Examples of Assessment Guidelines

KNOWLEDGE COMPETENCIES

Demonstrate a knowledge and understanding of:

* The inputs to project initiation and the development of project scope.

* The tools and techniques utilized for formulating project scope.

* The outputs of project initiation and scope development—e.g., project charter, constraints, and assumptions.

PERFORMANCE COMPETENCIES

Demonstrate an ability to develop:

* Project Charter.

* Business Case.

Table 2-6. Project Scope Management: Initiating

_.2 Unit of Competence—Project Scope Management	
_.2.2 COMPETENCY CLUSTER: Planning	
Elements	**Performance Criteria**
_.2.2.1 Conduct Scope Planning (*PMBOK® Guide* 5.2)	.1 Evaluate and further define the project scope statement. .2 Determine the appropriate project or subproject level in which scope statement is needed. .3 Utilize a scope statement as the basis for future project decisions and for evaluating project tradeoffs. .4 Understand a scope statement as documentation of the agreement between the project team and customers or other stakeholders by focusing on key project deliverables and objectives. .5 Determine how and when to properly refine or modify the scope statement. .6 Develop a scope management plan. .7 Identify and evaluate the components of a scope management plan. .8 Identify and evaluate inputs to the scope management plan. .9 Identify and evaluate criteria for classifying and integrating project scope changes. .10 Understand the difference between a project scope management plan and a project scope statement (Knowledge only).
_.2.2.2 Conduct Scope Definition (*PMBOK® Guide* 5.3)	.1 Determine the appropriate level of decomposition detail for various WBS or parts of the WBS. .2 Develop a WBS, including the proper use of decomposition techniques. .3 Communicate the differences between a WBS and other types of breakdown structures. .4 Determine the utility of a WBS from similar past projects and standardized templates. .5 Determine the inputs of the project scope definition process. .6 Verify the correctness of the WBS, including Dictionary. .7 Identify specific Scope inclusions and exclusions.
Examples of Assessment Guidelines	

KNOWLEDGE COMPETENCIES

Demonstrate a knowledge and understanding of:

- The inputs to scope planning and definition.
- The tools and techniques utilized for the planning and definition of project scope.
- The outputs of scope planning and definition.
- Creation and use of the WBS.

PERFORMANCE COMPETENCIES

Demonstrate an ability to develop:

- Scope Statement.
- Scope Management Plan.
- WBS.

Table 2-7. Project Scope Management: Planning

_.2 Unit of Competence—Project Scope Management	
_.2.3 COMPETENCY CLUSTER: Executing	
Elements	**Performance Criteria**
_.2.3.1 **Execute Scope**	.1 Utilize the WBS to manage project deliverables. .2 Conduct work scope in accordance to plans. .3 Establish review/approval process for project deliverables.
Examples of Assessment Guidelines	

KNOWLEDGE COMPETENCIES

Demonstrate a knowledge and understanding of:

- The tools and techniques utilized for conducting scope execution.

- The outputs of scope execution.

PERFORMANCE COMPETENCIES

Demonstrate an ability to develop:

- Formal Acceptance Documentation.

Table 2-8. Project Scope Management: Executing

_.2 Unit of Competence—Project Scope Management	
_.2.4 COMPETENCY CLUSTER: Controlling	
Elements	**Performance Criteria**
_.2.4.1 Conduct Scope Verification (*PMBOK® Guide* 5.4)	.1 Participate in project inspections, reviews, audits, and walkthroughs. .2 Determine that work product/results are completed correctly. .3 Document product acceptance by stakeholders.
_.2.4.2 Conduct Scope Change Control (*PMBOK® Guide* 5.5)	.1 Evaluate the degree to which changes would affect the project scope. .2 Implement a scope change control system. .3 Evaluate alternatives to scope modifications. .4 Implement approved changes, manage related work tasks, and integrate approved scope changes into other control processes.
Examples of Assessment Guidelines	

KNOWLEDGE COMPETENCIES

Demonstrate a knowledge and understanding of:

- The inputs to scope change control and verification.
- The tools and techniques utilized for conducting scope change control and verification.
- The outputs of scope change control and verification.

PERFORMANCE COMPETENCIES

Demonstrate an ability to develop:

- Scope Change Requests.
- Corrective Action.
- Performance Reports.

Table 2-9. Project Scope Management: Controlling

_.2 Unit of Competence—Project Scope Management	
_.2.5 COMPETENCY CLUSTER: Closing	
Elements	**Performance Criteria**
_.2.5.1 **Conduct Project Closure with Regard to Scope**	.1 Identify causes of variances in project scope. .2 Identify the reasoning behind corrective actions chosen through scope change control. .3 Determine and document lessons learned with regard to scope. .4 Perform post-project review.
Examples of Assessment Guidelines	

KNOWLEDGE COMPETENCIES

Demonstrate a knowledge and understanding of:

• The inputs to project closure with regard to scope.

• The tools and techniques utilized for project closure.

• The outputs of project closure with regard to scope.

PERFORMANCE COMPETENCIES

Demonstrate an ability to develop:

• Lessons Learned.

• Post-Review Meeting Minutes/Notes.

Table 2-10. Project Scope Management: Closing

Unit of Competence—Project Time Management

_.3 Unit of Competence—Project Time Management	
_.3.1 COMPETENCY CLUSTER: Initiating	
Elements	**Performance Criteria**
_.3.1.1 **Preliminary Planning Activities**	.1 Identify customer expectations with regards to timing of delivery, major milestones, and any schedule and delivery constraints.
	.2 Identify internal and external schedule constraints and influences.
	.3 Identify key project milestones.
Examples of Assessment Guidelines	

KNOWLEDGE COMPETENCIES

Demonstrate a knowledge and understanding of:

• The inputs of preplanning activities.

• The tools and techniques of preplanning activities.

• The outputs of preplanning activities.

PERFORMANCE COMPETENCIES

Demonstrate an ability to develop:

• Project Milestone Plan.

Table 2-11. Project Time Management: Initiating

_.3 Unit of Competence—Project Time Management	
_.3.2 COMPETENCY CLUSTER: Planning	
Elements	**Performance Criteria**
_.3.2.1 Conduct Activity Definition (*PMBOK® Guide* 6.1)	.1 Create an activity list using decomposition of the lowest level of the WBS. .2 Identify the appropriate level of WBS detail for the activity list. .3 Determine the inputs to the project activity definition process. .4 Validate the WBS by ensuring that performing all activities will complete all deliverables. .5 Utilize activity lists to verify that all activities are within the project scope and that the WBS is correct. .6 Identify missing deliverables or deliverables requiring clarification, using the WBS as part of the verification process.
_.3.2.2 Conduct Activity Sequencing (*PMBOK® Guide* 6.2)	.1 Determine interactivity dependencies. .2 Identify the relationships between project activities for activity sequencing. .3 Identify and document the types of interactivity dependencies within the project. .4 Construct a project network diagram. .5 Identify appropriate diagramming techniques. .6 Determine inputs to the activity sequencing process. .7 Complete activity lists and WBS updates, as well as updates of related supporting documentation. .8 Define missing activities or activities requiring clarification in the activity list during the development of the project network diagram.
_.3.2.3 Conduct Activity Duration Estimating (*PMBOK® Guide* 6.3)	.1 Develop activity duration estimates for project scheduling using various tools, such as analogous estimation techniques. .2 Utilize simulations (e.g., results of Monte Carlo analysis). .3 Estimate the number of work periods and possible work duration ranges. .4 Document the basis for activity duration estimates. .5 Develop activity duration estimates.
_.3.2.4 Conduct Schedule Development (*PMBOK® Guide* 6.4)	.1 Formulate project and resource calendars. .2 Identify activity leads, lags, and constraints. .3 Determine inputs to the project schedule development process. .4 Select and perform appropriate mathematical analysis, e.g., critical path method. .5 Identify Program Graphical Evaluation and Review Technique needs. .6 Identify Program Evaluation and Review Technique needs. .7 Understand the advantages and disadvantages of the different types of project schedule formats (Knowledge only). .8 Determine the completeness of a project schedule. .9 Develop a schedule management plan, including establishing a schedule baseline, documenting how schedule variances will be managed, identifying schedule change control system procedures, and defining appropriate performance measures. .10 Produce a baseline project schedule.

Table 2-12. Project Time Management: Planning (*Continues*)

Examples of Assessment Guidelines

KNOWLEDGE COMPETENCIES

Demonstrate a knowledge and understanding of:

- The inputs to activity definition, sequencing and estimating, and schedule development.
- The tools and techniques utilized for the definition, sequencing and estimating of activities, and the development of the project schedule.
- The outputs of activity definition, sequencing and estimating, and schedule development.

PERFORMANCE COMPETENCIES

Demonstrate an ability to develop:

- Activity List with Duration Estimates.
- Project Schedule—Baseline.
- Schedule Management Plan.
- Network Diagram.

Table 2-12. Project Time Management: Planning *(Continued)*

_.3 Unit of Competence—Project Time Management	
_.3.3 COMPETENCY CLUSTER: Executing	
Elements	**Performance Criteria**
_3.3.1 Implement Project Schedule	.1 Implement mechanisms to measure, record, and report progress of activities in relation to the agreed schedule and plans.
	.2 Conduct ongoing analysis of options to identify variances and forecast the impact of changes on the schedule.
	.3 Review progress throughout the project life cycle and implement agreed schedule changes to ensure consistency with changing scope, objectives, and constraints related to time and resource availability.
	.4 Develop and implement agreed responses to perceived, potential, or actual schedule changes, to maintain project objectives.

Examples of Assessment Guidelines

KNOWLEDGE COMPETENCIES

Demonstrate a knowledge and understanding of:

- The mechanisms for measuring, recording, and reporting progress of schedule activities.
- The tools and techniques for analyzing variances and forecasting schedule change impacts.
- The approaches for developing responses for perceived, potential, or actual schedule changes.

PERFORMANCE COMPETENCIES

Demonstrate an ability to develop:

- Schedule Progress Reports.
- Schedule Change Forecasts or Trends.
- Planned Responses for Dealing with Schedule Changes.

Table 2-13. Project Time Management: Executing

_.3 Unit of Competence—Project Time Management	
_.3.4 COMPETENCY CLUSTER: Controlling	
Elements	**Performance Criteria**
_.3.4.1 Conduct Schedule Control (*PMBOK® Guide* 6.5)	.1 Define the procedure by which the project schedule may be changed. .2 Implement a schedule change control system. .3 Integrate schedule activities with the overall change control system. .4 Determine the need for a schedule change. .5 Determine the magnitude of the schedule change and the need for reestablishing the baseline. .6 Determine overall plan adjustments resulting from schedule updates. .7 Determine the need for schedule fast tracking or crashing. .8 Initiate corrective actions to ensure that additional schedule changes are minimized. .9 Integrate approved schedule changes with other project control processes.
Examples of Assessment Guidelines	

KNOWLEDGE COMPETENCIES

Demonstrate a knowledge and understanding of:

- The inputs to schedule control.

- The tools and techniques utilized for controlling changes to the schedule.

- The outputs of schedule control.

PERFORMANCE COMPETENCIES

Demonstrate an ability to develop:

- Schedule Updates.

- Corrective Action.

Table 2-14. Project Time Management: Controlling

_.3 Unit of Competence—Project Time Management	
_.3.5 COMPETENCY CLUSTER: Closing	
Elements	**Performance Criteria**
_.3.5.1 **Conduct Project Closure with Regard to Time**	.1 Document lessons learned, including causes of activities leading to schedule changes, types of schedule changes, reasons for selecting specific corrective actions, and classification of schedule change causes for further analysis.
Examples of Assessment Guidelines	

KNOWLEDGE COMPETENCIES

Demonstrate a knowledge and understanding of:

• The inputs to project closure with regard to time.

• The tools and techniques utilized for project closure.

• The outputs of project closure with regard to time.

PERFORMANCE COMPETENCIES

Demonstrate an ability to develop:

• Lessons Learned.

Table 2-15. Project Time Management: Closing

_.4 Unit of Competence—Project Cost Management	
_.4.1 COMPETENCY CLUSTER: Initiating	
Elements	**Performance Criteria**
_.4.1.1 High-Level Budget Development Preparation	.1 Develop a cost benefit analysis. .2 Identify budget constraints. .3 Develop business case.
Examples of Assessment Guidelines	

KNOWLEDGE COMPETENCIES

Demonstrate a knowledge and understanding of:

- The inputs to budget preparation.
- The tools and techniques of budget and budget preparation.
- The outputs of budget preparation.

PERFORMANCE COMPETENCIES

Demonstrate an ability to develop:

- Cost Benefit Analysis.
- Business Case.

Table 2-16. Project Cost Management: Initiating

Unit of Competence—Project Cost Management

_.4 Unit of Competence—Project Cost Management	
_.4.2 COMPETENCY CLUSTER: Planning	
Elements	**Performance Criteria**
_.4.2.1 Conduct Resource Planning (*PMBOK® Guide* 7.1)	.1 Identify physical resources available to the project, including contracted resources. .2 Evaluate historical resource information related to similar projects. .3 Comply with organizational policies regarding resource usage and selection. .4 Determine and quantify resource needs using the WBS, scope statement, resource pool descriptions, historical information, and organizational polices. .5 Identify staff requirements/assignments through a process of defining the skill types required, defining the types of individuals/groups required, developing job/position descriptions, identifying training needs, and defining required time frames. .6 Develop staffing management plans for assessment and control of human-resource usage patterns. .7 Develop resource histograms. .8 Identify project material and equipment requirements. .9 Identify the completeness of a resource requirements document, and track individual resource requirements to WBS elements. .10 Develop a responsibility assignment matrix. .11 Utilize a resource requirements statement as a basis for acquiring resources and managing other cost activities, including cost budgeting. .12 Develop a resource management plan.
_.4.2.2 Conduct Cost Estimating (*PMBOK® Guide* 7.2)	.1 Develop project cost estimates at an appropriate level of detail. .2 Identify and evaluate inputs to the project cost-estimating process. .3 Understand the differences between cost estimating and cost pricing (Knowledge only). .4 Identify and document appropriate cost-estimating methods. .5 Evaluate inputs to the cost baseline development process. .6 Utilize multiple cost baselines to evaluate different aspects of project cost performance over time. .7 Verify that cost estimates are complete and associated with specific resource requirements. .8 Develop a cost management plan. .9 Develop a cost change control plan. .10 Identify performance measurement techniques.
_.4.2.3 Conduct Cost Budgeting (*PMBOK® Guide* 7.3)	.1 Allocate overall costs to individual activities. .2 Utilize a chart of accounts to associate quantitative cost assessments with related resource requirements. .3 Develop a cost baseline to determine cost performance.

Table 2-17. Project Cost Management: Planning *(Continues)*

Examples of Assessment Guidelines

KNOWLEDGE COMPETENCIES

Demonstrate a knowledge and understanding of:

- The inputs to resource planning and cost estimating and budgeting.
- The tools and techniques utilized for the planning of resources and the compilation of cost estimates and budgets.
- The outputs of resource planning and cost estimating and budgeting.

PERFORMANCE COMPETENCIES

Demonstrate an ability to develop/use:

- List of Resource Requirements.
- Cost Estimates.
- Cost Management Plan.
- Cost Baseline.
- Chart of Accounts.

Table 2-17. Project Cost Management: Planning *(Continued)*

_.4 Unit of Competence—Project Cost Management	
_.4.3 COMPETENCY CLUSTER: Executing	
Elements	**Performance Criteria**
_.4.3.1 **Execute Cost Baseline**	.1 Implement agreed financial management procedures and processes to monitor actual expenditure and to control costs.
	.2 Select and utilize cost analysis methods and tools to identify cost variations, evaluate options, and recommend actions to higher project authority.
	.3 Implement, monitor, and modify agreed actions to maintain financial and overall project objectives throughout the project life cycle.
Examples of Assessment Guidelines	

KNOWLEDGE COMPETENCIES

Demonstrate a knowledge and understanding of:

- The inputs to cost execution.
- The tools and techniques utilized for the baseline execution.

PERFORMANCE COMPETENCIES

Demonstrate an ability to monitor:

- Baseline Cost Execution.

Table 2-18. Project Cost Management: Executing

_.4 Unit of Competence—Project Cost Management	
_.4.4 COMPETENCY CLUSTER: Controlling	
Elements	**Performance Criteria**
_4.4.1 Conduct Cost Control (*PMBOK® Guide* 7.4)	.1 Implement a cost change control system. .2 Integrate cost changes within the overall change control system. .3 Implement cost controls. .4 Define and evaluate factors that may potentially cause cost changes. .5 Revise cost estimates, and evaluate the degree to which the cost baseline has changed using performance techniques such as earned value analysis. .6 Integrate approved cost changes with other project control processes. .7 Determine modifications needed to estimates for completion.
Examples of Assessment Guidelines	

KNOWLEDGE COMPETENCIES

Demonstrate a knowledge and understanding of:

- The inputs to cost control.
- The tools and techniques utilized for controlling changes to the cost baseline or budget.
- The outputs of cost control.

PERFORMANCE COMPETENCIES

Demonstrate an ability to develop:

- List of Revised Cost Estimates.
- List of Budget Updates.
- Estimate at Completion.

Table 2-19. Project Cost Management: Controlling

_.4 Unit of Competence—Project Cost Management	
_.4.5 COMPETENCY CLUSTER: Closing	
Elements	**Performance Criteria**
_.4.5.1 **Conduct Project Closure with Regard to Cost**	.1 Document lessons learned, including causes of activities leading to cost changes, types of cost changes, reasons for selecting specific corrective actions, and classification of cost changes for further analysis.
Examples of Assessment Guidelines	

KNOWLEDGE COMPETENCIES

Demonstrate a knowledge and understanding of:

- The inputs to project closure with regard to cost.

- The tools and techniques utilized for project closure.

- The outputs of project closure with regard to cost.

PERFORMANCE COMPETENCIES

Demonstrate an ability to develop:

- Lessons Learned.

Table 2-20. Project Cost Management: Closing

Unit of Competence—Project Quality Management

_.5 Unit of Competence—Project Quality Management	
_.5.1 COMPETENCY CLUSTER: Initiating	
Elements	**Performance Criteria**
_.5.1.1 Determine Quality Requirements	.1 Determine quality objectives, standards, and levels, with input from stakeholders and guidance of higher project authorities, to establish the basis for quality outcomes. .2 Determine the organization's quality policy. .3 Develop project quality policies.
Examples of Assessment Guidelines	

KNOWLEDGE COMPETENCIES

Demonstrate a knowledge and understanding of:

- The inputs to determining quality requirements.
- The impact the organization's quality policies have on determining quality requirements.
- The outputs of quality policies.

PERFORMANCE COMPETENCIES

Demonstrate an ability to develop:

- Quality Requirements Documentation.

Table 2-21. Project Quality Management: Initiating

_.5 Unit of Competence—Project Quality Management	
_.5.2 COMPETENCY CLUSTER: Planning	
Elements	**Performance Criteria**
_.5.2.1 **Conduct Quality Planning** (*PMBOK® Guide* 8.1)	.1 Develop project quality policies and ensure they are aligned with the organization's quality policy. .2 Utilize standard project quality tools and techniques. .3 Develop project quality metrics and performance checklists. .4 Develop a project quality management plan. .5 Evaluate project quality control, assurance, and improvement issues. .6 Communicate quality-related inputs of the project, the project's product, and the related effects on other project planning processes to the project's stakeholders.
Examples of Assessment Guidelines	

KNOWLEDGE COMPETENCIES

Demonstrate a knowledge and understanding of:

- The inputs to quality planning.
- The tools and techniques utilized for quality planning.
- The outputs of quality planning.

PERFORMANCE COMPETENCIES

Demonstrate an ability to develop:

- Quality Management Plan.
- Quality Checklist.
- Metrics Plan.

Table 2-22. Project Quality Management: Planning

.5 Unit of Competence—Project Quality Management	
_.5.3 COMPETENCY CLUSTER: Executing	
Elements	**Performance Criteria**
_.5.3.1 Conduct Quality Assurance (*PMBOK® Guide* 8.2)	.1 Perform project quality control testing and measurement. .2 Determine the benefits/costs of project quality efforts. .3 Document project quality outcomes in a format suitable for comparison and analysis. .4 Identify and implement actions needed to increase project effectiveness and efficiency. .5 Document lessons learned for improved performance. .6 Implement quality improvements using the project change control processes. .7 Execute project quality control, assurance, and improvement processes.
Examples of Assessment Guidelines	

KNOWLEDGE COMPETENCIES

Demonstrate a knowledge and understanding of:

- The inputs to quality assurance.

- The tools and techniques utilized for quality assurance.

- The outputs of quality assurance.

PERFORMANCE COMPETENCIES

Demonstrate an ability to develop:

- Mechanism for Quality Improvement.

- Metrics Report.

Table 2-23. Project Quality Management: Executing

_.5 Unit of Competence—Project Quality Management	
_.5.4 COMPETENCY CLUSTER: Controlling	
Elements	**Performance Criteria**
_5.4.1 Conduct Quality Control (*PMBOK® Guide* 8.3)	.1 Monitor specific project results to ensure compliance with requirements (relevant quality standards) using appropriate checklists. .2 Perform inspections, reviews, and walkthroughs to ensure that items are properly documented as accepted, rejected, or identified for rework. .3 Utilize techniques, including Pareto analysis, cause/effect diagrams, trend analysis, and statistical sampling for inspections. .4 Implement process adjustments to ensure quality improvement efforts. .5 Complete all quality-related documentation.
Examples of Assessment Guidelines	

KNOWLEDGE COMPETENCIES

Demonstrate a knowledge and understanding of:

- The inputs to quality control.

- The tools and techniques utilized for quality control.

- The outputs of quality control.

PERFORMANCE COMPETENCIES

Demonstrate an ability to develop:

- Acceptance Decisions.

- Reductions in Rework.

- Completed Checklists.

- Process Adjustments.

Table 2-24. Project Quality Management: Controlling

_.5 Unit of Competence—Project Quality Management	
_.5.5 COMPETENCY CLUSTER: Closing	
Elements	**Performance Criteria**
_.5.5.1 Conduct Project Closure with Regard to Quality	.1 Document lessons learned, including causes of activities leading to quality changes, types of quality changes, reasons for selecting specific corrective actions, and classification of quality change causes for further analysis.
Examples of Assessment Guidelines	

KNOWLEDGE COMPETENCIES

Demonstrate a knowledge and understanding of:

- The inputs to project closure with regard to quality.

- The tools and techniques utilized for project closure.

- The outputs of project closure with regard to quality.

PERFORMANCE COMPETENCIES

Demonstrate an ability to develop:

- Lessons Learned.

- Metrics Summary Report.

Table 2-25. Project Quality Management: Closing

Unit of Competence—Project Human Resources Management

_.6 Unit of Competence—Project Human Resources Management	
_.6.1 COMPETENCY CLUSTER: Initiating	
Elements	**Performance Criteria**
_.6.1.1 **Conduct Organizational Definition**	.1 Complete stakeholder needs analysis as a guide to the project planning process.
	.2 Identify the organizational structure (e.g., strong matrix and weak matrix) in order to determine project effects.
	.3 Identify specific organizational role/responsibility assignment processes.
Examples of Assessment Guidelines	

KNOWLEDGE COMPETENCIES

Demonstrate a knowledge and understanding of:

- The inputs to organizational definition.
- The tools and techniques utilized for the definition of HR/organizational requirements.
- The outputs of organizational definition.

PERFORMANCE COMPETENCIES

Demonstrate an ability to develop:

- Role and Responsibility Assignments.
- Organizational Breakdown Structure (OBS).

Table 2-26. Project Human Resources Management: Initiating

.6 Unit of Competence—Project Human Resources Management	
_.6.2 COMPETENCY CLUSTER: Planning	
Elements	**Performance Criteria**
_.6.2.1 Conduct Organizational Planning *(PMBOK® Guide 9.1)*	.1 Complete overall organizational planning processes. .2 Develop an organizational chart for project work. .3 Describe project effects of organizational units, technical interfaces, and the presence of different technical disciplines. .4 Utilize an OBS to evaluate unit responsibilities for specific work items on the project. .5 Develop a staffing management plan. .6 Develop project team policies and procedures.
_.6.2.2 Conduct Staff Acquisition *(PMBOK® Guide 9.2)*	.1 Determine human resource requirements for individual tasks with input from stakeholders and guidance from higher project authorities, to provide a basis for determining project staffing levels and competencies. .2 Establish project organization, structure, and directory to align individual and group competencies with project tasks. .3 Allocate project staff to and within the project or within the organization as directed by a higher project authority, to meet competency requirements throughout the project life cycle. .4 Communicate designated staff responsibilities, authority, and personal performance measurement criteria, to ensure clarity of understanding of the work and to provide a basis for ongoing assessment.
Examples of Assessment Guidelines	

KNOWLEDGE COMPETENCIES

Demonstrate a knowledge and understanding of:

- The inputs to organizational planning and staff acquisition.

- The tools and techniques utilized for organizational planning and staff acquisition.

- The outputs of organizational planning and staff acquisition.

PERFORMANCE COMPETENCIES

Demonstrate an ability to develop:

- Staffing Management Plan.

- Organization Chart.

- Project Directory.

Table 2-27. Project Human Resources Management: Planning

_.6 Unit of Competence—Project Human Resources Management	
_.6.3 COMPETENCY CLUSTER: Executing	
Elements	**Performance Criteria**
_.6.3.1 Conduct Team Development (*PMBOK® Guide* 9.3)	.1 Utilize project team policies and procedures. .2 Perform team-building activities. .3 Establish a collocated team (if possible). .4 Implement programs that enhance project team performance, including use of conflict/stress reduction techniques. .5 Develop rewards and recognition plan. .6 Implement rewards/recognitions according to plan.
Examples of Assessment Guidelines	

KNOWLEDGE COMPETENCIES

Demonstrate a knowledge and understanding of:

- The inputs to team development.
- The tools and techniques utilized for team development.
- The outputs of team development.

PERFORMANCE COMPETENCIES

Demonstrate an ability to develop:

- Performance Improvements.
- Input to Performance Appraisals.
- Rewards and Recognition Plan.

Table 2-28. Project Human Resources Management: Executing

_.6 Unit of Competence—Project Human Resources Management	
_.6.4 COMPETENCY CLUSTER: Controlling	
Elements	**Performance Criteria**
_.6.4.1 **Manage Human Resources**	.1 Manage changes in organizational plans.
	.2 Monitor results of team-building activities.
	.3 Monitor effectiveness of programs for enhancing project team performance.
	.4 Monitor rewards and recognition plan.
Examples of Assessment Guidelines	

KNOWLEDGE COMPETENCIES

Demonstrate a knowledge and understanding of:

- The inputs to organizational planning and staff acquisition.
- The tools and techniques utilized for organizational planning and staff acquisition.
- The outputs of organizational planning and staff acquisition.

PERFORMANCE COMPETENCIES

Demonstrate an ability to update:

- Staffing Management Plan.
- Organization Chart.
- Project Directory.

Table 2-29. Project Human Resources Management: Controlling

©2002 Project Management Institute, Four Campus Boulevard, Newtown Square, PA 19073-3299 USA

_.6 Unit of Competence—Project Human Resources Management	
_.6.5 COMPETENCY CLUSTER: Closing	
Elements	**Performance Criteria**
_.6.5.1 **Conduct Project Closure with Regard to HR Management**	.1 Implement transition activities to return resources to parent organization. .2 Document lessons learned, including causes of activities leading to changes, types of changes, reasons for selecting specific corrective actions, and classification of change causes for further analysis.
Examples of Assessment Guidelines	

KNOWLEDGE COMPETENCIES

Demonstrate a knowledge and understanding of:

*   The inputs to project closure with regard to HR.

*   The tools and techniques utilized for project closure.

*   The outputs of project closure with regard to HR.

PERFORMANCE COMPETENCIES

Demonstrate an ability to develop:

*   Transition Plans.

*   Lessons Learned.

Table 2-30. Project Human Resources Management: Closing

Unit of Competence—Project Communications Management

_.7 Unit of Competence—Project Communications Management	
_.7.1 COMPETENCY CLUSTER: Initiating	
Elements	**Performance Criteria**
_.7.1.1 **Preliminary Communications Planning**	.1 Identify the project/organization communications policies.
Examples of Assessment Guidelines	

KNOWLEDGE COMPETENCIES

Demonstrate a knowledge and understanding of:

- The inputs to communications planning.

- The tools and techniques utilized for communications planning.

- The outputs of communications planning.

PERFORMANCE COMPETENCIES

Demonstrate an ability to develop:

- Supporting Detail for Communications Management Plan.

Table 2-31. Project Communications Management: Initiating

_.7 Unit of Competence—Project Communications Management	
_.7.2 COMPETENCY CLUSTER: Planning	
Elements	**Performance Criteria**
_.7.2.1 Conduct Communications Planning (*PMBOK® Guide* 10.1)	.1 Determine the detailed information requirements of the project stakeholders and the project/organization. .2 Establish project information storage system. .3 Document stakeholder logistic issues. .4 Identify external information needs. .5 Determine format of the information needs. .6 Develop feedback routines to ensure two-way communication. .7 Identify the immediacy of the need. .8 Determine the technologies or methods used to transmit information. .9 Identify the project team experience in order to conduct communications technology-related training. .10 Identify the methods needed to transmit non-routine communications. .11 Develop a communications management plan. .12 Establish project status reporting process and cycle. .13 Determine the requirements for project time reporting. .14 Select a suitable time-reporting mechanism.
Examples of Assessment Guidelines	

KNOWLEDGE COMPETENCIES

Demonstrate a knowledge and understanding of:
- The inputs to communications planning.
- The tools and techniques utilized for communications planning.
- The outputs of communications planning.

PERFORMANCE COMPETENCIES

Demonstrate an ability to develop:
- Project Files.
- Mechanisms for Obtaining Feedback from Stakeholders.
- Communications Management Plan.

Table 2-32. Project Communications Management: Planning

_.7 Unit of Competence—Project Communications Management	
_.7.3 COMPETENCY CLUSTER: Executing	
Elements	**Performance Criteria**
_.7.3.1 Conduct Information Distribution (*PMBOK® Guide* 10.2)	.1 Implement a project information distribution system. .2 Implement a project information retrieval system. .3 Respond to expected and unexpected information requests. .4 Maintain project records.
_.7.3.2 Implement Project Time Reporting	.1 Execute requirements and processes for time reporting to all project stakeholders. .2 Include time-reporting data in regular progress reports.
Examples of Assessment Guidelines	

KNOWLEDGE COMPETENCIES

Demonstrate a knowledge and understanding of:

- The inputs to information distribution and time reporting.

- The tools and techniques utilized for information distribution and time reporting.

- The outputs of information distribution and time reporting.

PERFORMANCE COMPETENCIES

Demonstrate an ability to develop:

- Project Records.

- Project Progress Reports.

- Analysis of Planned versus Actual Hours.

Table 2-33. Project Communications Management: Executing

_.7 Unit of Competence—Project Communications Management	
_.7.4 COMPETENCY CLUSTER: Controlling	
Elements	**Performance Criteria**
_.7.4.1 Conduct Project Performance Reporting (*PMBOK® Guide* 10.3)	.1 Implement project performance reviews. .2 Generate and disseminate status, progress, and forecast reports to appropriate stakeholders, e.g., variance, trend, earned value, etc. .3 Create change requests based on performance reports. .4 Monitor compliance to ensure that timely and accurate data are available.
Examples of Assessment Guidelines	

KNOWLEDGE COMPETENCIES

Demonstrate a knowledge and understanding of:

- The inputs to performance reporting.
- The tools and techniques utilized for performance reporting.
- The outputs of performance reporting.

PERFORMANCE COMPETENCIES

Demonstrate an ability to develop:

- Performance Reports.
- Change Requests.

Table 2-34. Project Communications Management: Controlling

_.7 Unit of Competence—Project Communications Management	
_.7.5 COMPETENCY CLUSTER: Closing	
Elements	**Performance Criteria**
_.7.5.1 Conduct Administrative Closeout (*PMBOK® Guide* 10.4)	.1 Define and implement closure at the end phase of the project by collecting all project records, documenting the degree to which each project phase was properly closed after its completion, and verifying all project results in preparation for formal acceptance. .2 Document performance measures resulting from performance reviews, as well as variance, trend, and earned value analyses. .3 Review final specifications, and analyze project success and effectiveness. .4 Document the final project scope. .5 Document lessons learned. .6 Formalize the acceptance/sign-off of the product by the sponsor, client, or customer. .7 Perform final appraisal reviews of team members. .8 Archive relevant project documentation.
Examples of Assessment Guidelines	

KNOWLEDGE COMPETENCIES

Demonstrate a knowledge and understanding of:

- The inputs to project closure with regard to communications.

- The tools and techniques utilized for project closure.

- The outputs of project closure with regard to communications.

PERFORMANCE COMPETENCIES

Demonstrate an ability to develop:

- Lessons Learned.

- Project Closure Documentation.

- Project Archives.

Table 2-35. Project Communications Management: Closing

Unit of Competence—Project Risk Management

_.8 Unit of Competence—Project Risk Management	
_.8.1 COMPETENCY CLUSTER: Initiating	
Elements	**Performance Criteria**
_.8.1.1 **Conduct Preliminary Risk Planning**	.1 Identify and review organization's risk management policies and procedures.
	.2 Identify risk tolerance levels of stakeholders.
	.3 Identify preliminary risk.
Examples of Assessment Guidelines	

KNOWLEDGE COMPETENCIES

Demonstrate a knowledge and understanding of:
- The inputs to preliminary risk planning.
- The tools and techniques utilized for risk planning.
- The outputs of preliminary risk planning.

PERFORMANCE COMPETENCIES

Demonstrate an ability to develop:
- Preliminary Risk Assessment Matrix.

Table 2-36. Project Risk Management: Initiating

Elements	Performance Criteria

_.8 Unit of Competence—Project Risk Management

_.8.2 COMPETENCY CLUSTER: Planning

Elements	Performance Criteria
_.8.2.1 Develop Risk Management Plan (*PMBOK® Guide* 11.1)	.1 Identify roles, responsibilities, and levels of authority for risk management decision-making. .2 Review and expand preliminary risk assessment matrix. .3 Develop risk management plan. .4 Develop the process by which risk identification and quantification will be maintained.
_.8.2.2 Conduct Risk Identification (*PMBOK® Guide* 11.2)	.1 Identify potential project risk events. .2 Identify the sources of possible internal/external risk events. .3 Develop flowcharts to determine the causes and effects of risk. .4 Classify potential risk events, the ranges of possible outcomes, and risk interactions anticipated during various project phases. .5 Identify risk symptoms or triggers.
_.8.2.3 Conduct Qualitative Risk Analysis (*PMBOK® Guide* 11.3)	.1 Document the manifestations of risk events. .2 Confirm stakeholder risk tolerances. .3 Estimate risk event probability, consequence, and frequency. .4 Estimate risk event value and related range of possible project costs. .5 Develop probability/impact risk rating matrix. .6 Develop list of prioritized risks. .7 Determine overall risk ranking for the project.
_.8.2.4 Conduct Quantitative Risk Analysis (*PMBOK® Guide* 11.4)	.1 Conduct risk interviews with project stakeholders and subject-matter experts to support quantitative risk analysis. .2 Conduct sensitivity analysis on probable risk events. .4 Utilize simulation to analyze the behavior/performance of the project system. .5 Develop decision tree analysis to depict key interactions. .6 Communicate the limitations of risk quantification in order to avoid false impressions of risk assessment reliability. .7 Prepare a probabilistic risk analysis for the project.
_.8.2.5 Conduct Risk Response Planning (*PMBOK® Guide* 11.5)	.1 Work with stakeholders to develop risk responses. .2 Determine procurement feasibility as a risk reduction tool. .3 Develop contingency plans, implementation criteria, and alternative strategies. .4 Determine insurance coverage needs. .5 Determine risk events warranting responses. .6 Assign risk owners. .7 Identify other processes affected by risk planning iterations. .8 Estimate the Price of Non-Conformance to identified risks. .9 Determine and document the appropriateness of specific risk event strategies. .10 Describe potential differences in risk event estimates depending on the project phase. .11 Determine contingency reserve amounts needed. .12 Develop a risk response plan.

Table 2-37. Project Risk Management: Planning (*Continues*)

Examples of Assessment Guidelines

KNOWLEDGE COMPETENCIES

Demonstrate a knowledge and understanding of:

- The inputs to risk planning and response development.
- The tools and techniques utilized for the evaluation of potential risk events and the planning and development of risk responses.
- The outputs of risk planning and response development.

PERFORMANCE COMPETENCIES

Demonstrate an ability to develop:

- Risk Management Plan.
- Contingency Plans.
- Contractual Agreements.
- Risk Assessment Matrix.
- Probability Impact Matrix.
- Sensitivity Analysis.
- Decision Tree Analysis.
- Risk Response Plan.

Table 2-37. Project Risk Management: Planning *(Continued)*

_.8 Unit of Competence—Project Risk Management	
_.8.3 COMPETENCY CLUSTER: Executing	
Elements	**Performance Criteria**
_8.3.1 Execute Risk Response Plan	.1 Implement risk response plan including preventive actions as necessary.
	.2 Initiate and manage change requests as a response to risk events.
	.3 Manage change to risk response plan as a result of evolving circumstances.

Examples of Assessment Guidelines

KNOWLEDGE COMPETENCIES

Demonstrate a knowledge and understanding of:

- The inputs to execution of risk response plans.
- The tools and techniques utilized for execution of risk responses.
- The outputs of risk response execution.

PERFORMANCE COMPETENCIES

Demonstrate an ability to update:

- Project Risk Response Plans.

Table 2-38. Project Risk Management: Executing

_.8 Unit of Competence—Project Risk Management	
_.8.4 COMPETENCY CLUSTER: Controlling	
Elements	**Performance Criteria**
_.8.4.1 **Conduct Risk Monitoring and Control** (*PMBOK® Guide* 11.6)	.1 Create workarounds for unplanned risk events. .2 Implement workarounds for unplanned risk events. .3 Quantify actual risk events (for comparison and evaluation with the risk plan). .4 Complete risk event updates as part of the project control process. .5 Complete risk response plan updates, including adjustments to risk probabilities and risk values.
Examples of Assessment Guidelines	

KNOWLEDGE COMPETENCIES

Demonstrate a knowledge and understanding of:

- The inputs to risk response control.
- The tools and techniques utilized for conducting risk response control.
- The outputs of risk response control.

PERFORMANCE COMPETENCIES

Demonstrate an ability to develop:

- Updates to Risk Response Plan.
- Corrective Actions.
- Workarounds.

Table 2-39. Project Risk Management: Controlling

_.8 Unit of Competence—Project Risk Management	
_.8.5 COMPETENCY CLUSTER: Closing	
Elements	**Performance Criteria**
_.8.5.1 **Conduct Project Closure with Regard to Risk Management**	.1 Review project outcomes to determine effectiveness of risk management processes and procedures. .2 Identify, document, and report risk issues to recommend improvements to a higher project authority for application in future projects.
Examples of Assessment Guidelines	

KNOWLEDGE COMPETENCIES

Demonstrate a knowledge and understanding of:

- The inputs to project closure with regard to risk.
- The tools and techniques utilized for project closure.
- The outputs of project closure with regard to risk.

PERFORMANCE COMPETENCIES

Demonstrate an ability to develop:

- Lessons Learned.

Table 2-40. Project Risk Management: Closing

Unit of Competence—Project Procurement Management

_.9 Unit of Competence—Project Procurement Management	
_.9.1 COMPETENCY CLUSTER: Initiation	
Elements	**Performance Criteria**
_.9.1.1 Preliminary Procurement Planning	.1 Identify and review organization's procurement policies and procedures.
Examples of Assessment Guidelines	

KNOWLEDGE COMPETENCIES

Demonstrate a knowledge and understanding of:

- The inputs to preliminary procurement planning.

- The tools and techniques utilized for procurement planning.

- The outputs of procurement planning.

PERFORMANCE COMPETENCIES

Demonstrate an ability to develop:

- Preliminary Procurement Plan.

Table 2-41. Project Procurement Management: Initiating

_.9 Unit of Competence—Project Procurement Management	
_.9.2 COMPETENCY CLUSTER: Planning	
Elements	**Performance Criteria**
_.9.2.1 Conduct Procurement Planning (*PMBOK® Guide* 12.1)	.1 Utilize make-or-buy analysis to identify which project needs are best met by procuring products and/or services. .2 Communicate inputs to the procurement planning process. .3 Determine the contract types available for project procurement planning purposes. .4 Develop rating and scoring evaluation criteria for project procurement planning purposes. .5 Determine the different types of procurement documents. .6 Develop the procurement management plan. .7 Develop a procurement statement of work.
_.9.2.2 Conduct Solicitation Planning (*PMBOK® Guide* 12.2)	.1 Obtain information from established sources capable of fulfilling procurement requirements to determine the extent to which project objectives can be met. .2 Implement and communicate established selection processes and selection criteria to stakeholders and prospective contractors to ensure fair competition. .3 Obtain approvals from higher project authority to enable formal discussions to be conducted.
Examples of Assessment Guidelines	

KNOWLEDGE COMPETENCIES

Demonstrate a knowledge and understanding of:

- The inputs to procurement and solicitation planning.

- The tools and techniques utilized for procurement and solicitation planning.

- The outputs of procurement and solicitation planning.

PERFORMANCE COMPETENCIES

Demonstrate an ability to develop:

- Procurement Management Plan.

- Procurement Statement of Work.

Table 2-42. Project Procurement Management: Planning

_.9 Unit of Competence—Project Procurement Management	
_.9.3 COMPETENCY CLUSTER: Executing	
Elements	**Performance Criteria**
_.9.3.1 Conduct Solicitation (*PMBOK® Guide* 12.3)	.1 Conduct solicitation activities to obtain bids/proposals from prospective sellers. .2 Conduct bidder/contractor conferences. .3 Develop advertising to support solicitation. .4 Collect proposals for evaluation.
_.9.3.2 Conduct Source Selection/ Contract Development (*PMBOK® Guide* 12.4)	.1 Define and utilize project payment/invoicing terms. .2 Determine project changes, delays, and implementation of termination clauses when appropriate. .3 Rely upon methods to identify project warranties, liabilities, indemnity, and insurance clause-related activities. .4 Conduct contract negotiations. .5 Quantify qualitative data as an aid in source selection. .6 Evaluate and select source of procured resources, and award contract.
_.9.3.3 Conduct Contract Administration (*PMBOK® Guide* 12.5)	.1 Complete payment reviews/approvals. .2 Review contractors' change status reports and dissemination of contractual changes to appropriate parties. .3 Integrate contract administration within the broader context of the project plan, quality control processes, and the overall project performance reporting systems.
Examples of Assessment Guidelines	

KNOWLEDGE COMPETENCIES

Demonstrate a knowledge and understanding of:

- The inputs to source selection/contract development.

- The tools and techniques utilized for source selection/contract development.

- The outputs of source selection/contract development.

PERFORMANCE COMPETENCIES

Demonstrate an ability to develop:

- Procurement Documentation.

- Evaluation Criteria.

- Contract.

- Contract Administration Correspondence.

Table 2-43. Project Procurement Management: Executing

_.9 Unit of Competence—Project Procurement Management	
_.9.4 COMPETENCY CLUSTER: Controlling	
Elements	**Performance Criteria**
_.9.4.1 **Manage and Review Contract Performance**	.1 Review contractor costs, schedules, and technical performance levels.
	.2 Implement a contract change control system.
Examples of Assessment Guidelines	

KNOWLEDGE COMPETENCIES

Demonstrate a knowledge and understanding of:
- The inputs to contract/procurement controls.
- The tools and techniques utilized for controlling contracts/procurement.
- The outputs of contract/procurement control.

PERFORMANCE COMPETENCIES

Demonstrate an ability to:
- Manage Changes to Contracts.

Table 2-44. Project Procurement Management: Controlling

_.9 Unit of Competence—Project Procurement Management	
_.9.5 COMPETENCY CLUSTER: Closing	
Elements	**Performance Criteria**
_.9.5.1 **Conduct Contract Closeout** (*PMBOK® Guide* 12.6)	.1 Determine the quality and completeness of the contract file.
	.2 Incorporate administrative closeout into contract closeout process, including updating of records based upon final contract results, indexing and archiving of contract information, and identifying special case closeouts, such as early terminations.
	.3 Verify contract documentation outlining the completion and quality of work results.
	.4 Obtain formal acceptance from customer(s) regarding contract completion.
Examples of Assessment Guidelines	

KNOWLEDGE COMPETENCIES

Demonstrate a knowledge and understanding of:
- The inputs to project closure with regard to procurement.
- The tools and techniques utilized for project closure.
- The outputs of project closure with regard to procurement.

PERFORMANCE COMPETENCIES

Demonstrate an ability to develop:
- Formal Acceptance and Closure Documentation.
- Lessons Learned.

Table 2-45. Project Procurement Management: Closing

Section 3

Personal Competencies

As detailed in Section 1 of this publication, Personal Competencies are those personal characteristics (core personality, behavior, and attitudes) underlying a person's capability to manage a project.

The Personal Competencies presented here are those considered to best represent the personal characteristics required of a competent project manager in any nature or type of project. They have been derived from the Competency Dictionary (known as the Spencer Model) developed by Lyle and Signe Spencer (1993) and adapted to fit the technical needs of the *PMCD Framework*.

It can be seen from these Competencies that not only do they address core personality issues of an individual (such as self-control, self-confidence, and so on), but also factors that would apply generally in the workplace and, in particular, to the management of projects and organizational awareness.

Purpose of the Personal Competencies

The **Personal Competencies,** outlined in this section of the *PMCD Framework,* provide a basis for guidance, to develop the instruments required for assessing these competencies. As with the Project Management Knowledge/Performance Competencics, in order to be judged fully competent—as defined by the units of competence outlined for this dimension of the *PMCD Framework*—a project manager would have to be viewed as satisfying the performance criteria defining the individual elements of competence. Again, it is the generic construction of the *PMCD Framework* that helps to ensure that project manager competence in individuals will be transferable across organizations and industries. When constructing their assessment instruments, organizations should keep this generic construction in mind as they determine the overall relevance of the discrete elements and performance criteria within this section of the *PMCD Framework*.

It is envisioned that both individuals and organizations will be able to use this part of the *PMCD Framework* as a basis for professional development. Mechanisms for the assessment of individuals in this dimension could include a full 360-degree feedback process, as well as individual Peer and/or Self-Reviews.

The Personal Competencies are organized into six (6) units of competence representing groupings of distinguishing competencies. These are:
• Achievement and Action
• Helping and Human Service
• Impact and Influence
• Managerial
• Cognitive
• Personal Effectiveness.

Within each unit, competencies relating to similar actions or behavior are grouped together to form the competency clusters. Each competency cluster is broken down into one (1) or more elements reflecting the level of autonomy, drive, or urgency displayed, related to the competency. Performance criteria describe the behavior expected around the competency.

The *PMCD Framework* provides the standards required to perform assessment and, subsequently, the necessary design mechanism for organizations to develop these instruments, programs, and specifications. It provides the foundation for a methodology to achieve competence (see Section 4), which can be applied by both individuals and organizations.

As previously described in Section 1, the various Units of Competence can be represented in tabular format. On the following pages, Tables 3-1 through 3-6 utilize such a format, wherein each pertains to a different Unit of Competence, along with their associated Competency Clusters. Each of the Competency Clusters is further broken down into pertinent Elements and Performance Criteria. Note that each table also utilizes the numbering scheme originally detailed in Section 1.

Unit of Competence—Achievement and Action

B.1 Unit of Competence—Achievement and Action	
B.1.1 COMPETENCY CLUSTER: Achievement Orientation Achievement Orientation is a concern for working well, or for competing against, a standard of excellence.	
Element	**Performance Criteria**
B.1.1.1 **Operates with Intensity to Achieve Project Goals**	.1 Focuses on task(s) and standards of excellence set by relevant project stakeholders.
	.2 Strives to do job well, reaching goals set by project stakeholders.
	.3 Controls project risk proactively.
	.4 Sets high performance standards for self-acting as a role model for team.
B.1.1.2 **Motivates Project Stakeholders in a Positive Way**	.1 Strives to ensure that expectations of all stakeholders are achieved.
	.2 Drives increased effectiveness of the project team and the way it does business.
B.1.1.3 **Provides New Solutions in Planning and Delivering Projects**	.1 Performs innovative actions to improve performance of the project team.
B.1.1.4 **Operates with Individual Integrity and Personal Professionalism**	.1 Adheres to all legal requirements.
	.2 Works within a recognized set of ethical standards.
	.3 Discloses to all stakeholders any possible conflict of interest.
	.4 Neither offers nor accepts inappropriate payments or any other items for personal gain.
	.5 Maintains and respects confidentiality of sensitive information.
B.1.2 COMPETENCY CLUSTER: Concern for Order, Quality, and Accuracy Concern for order reflects an underlying drive to reduce uncertainty in the surrounding environment.	
Element	**Performance Criteria**
B.1.2.1 **Manages Projects in an Ordered, Accurate Way**	.1 Works with others to clarify project scope, roles, expectations, tasks, and data requirements.
	.2 Manages progress of the project against scope, quality, time, and cost baselines including approved changes.
	.3 Checks to ensure accuracy of data provided by others and to ensure that correct processes are followed.
B.1.2.2 **Provides Accurate and Truthful Information**	.1 Provides accurate information concerning own qualifications and experience.
	.2 Provides accurate information for estimates, actual and expected results, and risks to stakeholders.

Table 3-1. Achievement and Action Unit of Competence *(Continues)*

B.1 Unit of Competence—Achievement and Action	

B.1.3 COMPETENCY CLUSTER: Initiative

Initiative is the preference for taking action. It is doing more than is required or expected in the job, doing things that no one has requested, which will improve or enhance project results and avoid problems, or finding or creating new opportunities.

Element	Performance Criteria
B.1.3.1 Takes Initiative When Required	.1 Shows persistence in own actions—does not give up easily when things do not go smoothly. Takes direct action to address problems.
	.2 Addresses current opportunities or problems by taking positive actions to capitalize on opportunities or address present problems.
	.3 Acts quickly and decisively in a crisis where the norm is to wait, "study," and hope problem will resolve itself.
B.1.3.2 Takes Accountability for and Delivers Project	.1 Works independently and completes assignments without supervision.
	.2 Takes accountability for project outcome.
B.1.3.3 Seeks New Opportunities	.1 Looks for opportunities to add value for the client and one's own organization.
	.2 Seizes relevant opportunities as they emerge.
	.3 Consolidates opportunity or passes it to the organization.
B.1.3.4 Strives for Best Practice	.1 Enhances own knowledge and application of project management tools and techniques.
	.2 Shares lessons learned, best practices, etc. with project stakeholders.

B.1.4 COMPETENCY CLUSTER: Information Seeking

Information Seeking is an underlying curiosity, a desire to know more about things, people, or issues. It implies making an effort to get more information, not accepting situations "at face value."

Element	Performance Criteria
B.1.4.1 Ensures Information Used to Manage Project is Complete and Accurate	.1 Gets out personally to see for oneself. Questions those closest to the problem when others might ignore these people.
	.2 Asks probing questions to get at the root cause of a situation or a problem.
	.3 Calls on or contacts others, who are not personally involved, to get their perspectives, background information, or experience. (This is often through personal networking.)
	.4 Makes a systematic effort over a limited period of time to obtain needed data or feedback.
	.5 Reviews documentation on previous projects to incorporate lessons learned.
	.6 Seeks out appropriate Subject-Matter Experts for their knowledge.
	.7 Demonstrates persistence in tracking down information. Does not back down in the face of adversity or resistance.

Table 3-1. Achievement and Action Unit of Competence *(Continued)*

Unit of Competence—Helping and Human Service

B.2 Unit of Competence—Helping and Human Service	
B.2.1 COMPETENCY CLUSTER: Customer Service Orientation Customer Service Orientation implies a desire to help or serve others, to meet their needs. It means focusing efforts on discovering and meeting the customer or client needs.	
Element	**Performance Criteria**
B.2.1.1 Represents the Client Inside the Project	.1 Follows through on client inquiries, requests, and complaints. .2 Maintains clear communications with client regarding mutual expectations. .3 Monitors client satisfaction. Distributes helpful information to clients and gives friendly, cheerful service. .4 Acts to make things better. Makes concrete attempts to add value to client and to make things better for the client in some way. .5 Takes accountability for client satisfaction. .6 Provides as much service as possible before passing responsibility to another person. .7 Remains engaged to ensure that clients' needs are met. .8 Balances competing stakeholder interests striving for fair resolution.
B.2.1.2 Takes Initiatives to Provide Excellent Client Service	.1 Takes initiative to resolve client concerns. .2 Engages the client proactively; takes positive action to ensure that needs are met.
B.2.2 COMPETENCY CLUSTER: Interpersonal Understanding Interpersonal Understanding implies wanting to understand other people. It is the ability to hear accurately and understand the unspoken or partly expressed thoughts, feelings, and concerns of others.	
Element	**Performance Criteria**
B.2.2.1 Strives to Understand All Project Stakeholders' Thoughts, Feelings, and Concerns	.1 Strives to understand both the present emotions and explicit content of communications from project stakeholders. .2 Strives to understand underlying problems, and the reasons for someone's ongoing or long-term feelings, behaviors, or concerns. Objectively presents a balanced view of someone's specific strengths and weaknesses.
B.2.2.2 Listens and Responds to Others	.1 Picks up clues to others' feelings or meanings, and uses this understanding to explain others' past behaviors, understand current behaviors, and anticipate future behaviors. .2 Listens actively.

Table 3-2. Helping and Human Service Unit of Competence

Unit of Competence—Impact and Influence

B.3 Unit of Competence—Impact and Influence	
B.3.1 COMPETENCY CLUSTER: Impact and Influence Impact and Influence expresses an intention to persuade, convince, influence, or impress others in order to get them to support the speaker's agenda or to have a specific impact or effect on others.	
Element	**Performance Criteria**
B.3.1.1 Takes Appropriate Actions to Influence Others	.1 Takes multiple step actions to persuade, including careful preparation of data, or provides two or more different options in a presentation or discussion.
	.2 Adapts presentation or discussion to better fit the environment or setting of the presentation or meeting.
	.3 Uses experts or third parties to influence or persuade others to support one's actions, or to have a specific impact on the actions of other stakeholders involved in the situation.
B.3.1.2 Influences Across Projects and Organizations	.1 Models desired behavior to influence the work unit or project team.
	.2 Uses data and/or personal confidence in project proposals to positively influence key project stakeholders.
	.3 Strives to establish integrity within the project, the organization and externally.
B.3.1.3 Understands and Influences Project Team Members	.1 Takes time to learn what motivates performance in each project team member.
	.2 Rewards performance according to each member's value system.
	.3 Communicates the strategic value of the project to the team.
B.3.2 COMPETENCY CLUSTER: Organizational Awareness Organizational Awareness refers to the individual's ability to understand the power relationships in one's own organization or in other organizations (customers, suppliers, and so on). It includes the ability to identify who are the real decision-makers and the individuals who can influence them.	
Element	**Performance Criteria**
B.3.2.1 Understands the Organization	.1 Understands both the formal and informal structure or hierarchy of an organization, including the "chain of command," key actors, and decision-makers, and uses this understanding to influence support to accomplish goals and objectives of the project.
	.2 Understands the climate and culture of the organization and recognizes the unspoken organizational constraints—what is and is not possible at certain times or in certain positions.
B.3.2.2 Understands the Project	.1 Understands all issues relating to the project, the project team, and project stakeholders' organizations.
B.3.3 COMPETENCY CLUSTER: Relationship Building Relationship Building is working to build or maintain positive relationships or networks of contacts with people who are, or might someday be, useful in achieving work-related goals.	
Element	**Performance Criteria**
B.3.3.1 Builds and Maintains Suitable Relationships with Project Stakeholders	.1 Maintains formal working relationships; most contacts are work-related largely confined to work-related matters but not necessarily formal in tone, style, or structure.
	.2 Extends some contacts to informal or casual relationships at work—chats about children, sports, news, and so on.
B.3.3.2 Establishes and Maintains Relationships at the Right Level Inside and Outside the Organizations	.1 Maintains a network of relationships, which extends through all levels of the work unit or project team.
	.2 Navigates quickly through network to gain support to move project forward.

Table 3-3. Impact and Influence Unit of Competence

Unit of Competence—Managerial

B.4 Unit of Competence—Managerial	
B.4.1 COMPETENCY CLUSTER: Teamwork and Cooperation Teamwork and Cooperation implies a genuine intention to work cooperatively with others, to be part of a team, to work together, as opposed to working separately or competitively.	
Element	**Performance Criteria**
B.4.1.1 Builds Team Orientation Within the Project	.1 Expresses positive expectations of others directly involved in the project. Speaks to team members in positive terms.
	.2 Shows respect for others' intelligence by appealing to reason.
	.3 Genuinely values input and expertise of others on the team and is willing to learn from others (especially subordinates).
	.4 Publicly credits others who have performed well. Encourages and empowers others on the project team, making them feel strong and a true contributor to overall project success.
	.5 Does not hide or attempt to avoid conflict, but rather resolves it by bringing conflict within the immediate project team into the open and then encouraging or facilitating a beneficial resolution of the conflict.
B.4.1.2 Molds Core Project Stakeholders into a Team	.1 Establishes as a team those project team members with a direct reporting relationship to the project manager.
B.4.1.3 Undertakes Team-Building Activities	.1 Takes much more than routine action, on own time or over an extended period of time, to foster teamwork among all team members.
B.4.2 COMPETENCY CLUSTER: Developing Others Developing Others is a special version of impact and influence in which the intent is to teach or to foster the development of one or several other people. The essence of this competency lies in the developmental intent and effect rather than in a formal role.	
Element	**Performance Criteria**
B.4.2.1 Builds a Project Culture Where Personal Development Is Encouraged	.1 Expresses positive expectations of others regarding their abilities or potentials, even in "difficult" cases. Believes others want to and can learn.
	.2 Gives detailed instructions and/or on-the-job demonstrations telling how to do the task or making specific helpful suggestions.
	.3 Gives specific positive or mixed feedback for developmental purposes in a timely manner.
	.4 Gives reasons or rationale for actions or other support, such as expert advice to project team members, as a deliberate training strategy.
B.4.2.2 Develops Project Members to Effectively Build Project Culture	.1 Develops project team members with a direct reporting relationship to the project manager.

Table 3-4. Managerial Unit of Competence (Continues)

B.4.3 COMPETENCY CLUSTER: Team Leadership	
Team Leadership is the intention to take a role as leader of a team or other group. It implies a desire to lead others.	
Element	**Performance Criteria**
B.4.3.1 Demonstrates Leadership of the Project	.1 Informs a person affected by a decision about what is happening, ensuring that the group has all of the necessary information.
	.2 Uses authority fairly, making a personal effort to treat all team members equitably.
	.3 Promotes project team effectiveness by using strategies to promote morale and improve productivity.
	.4 Takes care of the project team, protecting it and its reputation vis-à-vis the larger organization or community at large. Ensures that the practical needs of the project team are met.
B.4.3.2 Leads the Project Team	.1 Leads directly those project team members with a direct reporting relationship to the project manager.
	.2 Invests extra time and effort over an extended period of time to lead the project team.
B.4.4 COMPETENCY CLUSTER: Directiveness: Assertiveness and Use of Positional Power	
Directiveness expresses the individual's intent to make others comply with one's wishes. Directive behavior has a theme or tone of "telling people what to do."	
Element	**Performance Criteria**
B.4.4.1 Uses Assertiveness When Necessary	.1 Speaks assertively, firmly saying, "No," to unreasonable requests, or setting limits for others' behavior.
	.2 Demands high performance, firmly setting standards for performance or quality.
	.3 Insists on compliance with procedures and policies.
B.4.4.2 Manages the Complete Project	.1 Takes accountability for project team members with a direct reporting relationship to the project manager.

Table 3-4. Managerial Unit of Competence (Continued)

Unit of Competence—Cognitive

B.5 Unit of Competence—Cognitive

B.5.1 COMPETENCY CLUSTER: Analytical Thinking Analytical Thinking is working through a situation by breaking it apart into smaller pieces, or tracing the implications of a situation in a step-by-step causal way.	
Element	**Performance Criteria**
B.5.1.1 Understands at a Suitable Level All Issues Associated with the Project	.1 Applies basic analytical techniques, such as breaking problems down into simple lists of activities, analyzing relationships among a few parts of a problem or situation, or making simple causal links (A causes B) or pro-and-con decisions.
	.2 Sets priorities for activities in order of importance.
	.3 Makes appropriate plans or analysis, systematically breaking down a complex problem or process into component parts. Uses several techniques to break apart complex problems to reach a solution; or makes long chains of causal connections.
	.4 Understands how actions taken on the project may impact other areas of the project, other projects in the organization or other organizational operations.
B.5.1.2 Facilitates Solutions Across All Issues Related to the Project	.1 Provides the framework so that solutions to problems or concerns involving the immediate project team are addressed.

B.5.2 COMPETENCY CLUSTER: Conceptual Thinking Conceptual Thinking is working through a situation or problem by putting the pieces together, seeing the large picture.	
Element	**Performance Criteria**
B.5.2.1 Sees the Project in a Holistic Way	.1 Observes discrepancies, trends, and interrelationships in data, or sees crucial differences between current situation and past situations.
	.2 Applies complex concepts (e.g., root-cause analysis, portfolio analysis, natural selection), or applies knowledge of past discrepancies, trends, and relationships to look at different situations.
	.3 Applies or modifies complex learned concepts or methods appropriately.
	.4 Simplifies complexities by pulling together ideas, issues, and observations into a single concept or a clear presentation.

Table 3-5. Cognitive Unit of Competence

Unit of Competence—Personal Effectiveness

B.6 Unit of Competence—Personal Effectiveness	
B.6.1 COMPETENCY CLUSTER: Self-Control Self-Control is the ability to keep emotions under control and restrain negative actions when tempted, when faced with opposition or hostility from others, or when working under conditions of stress.	
Element	**Performance Criteria**
B.6.1.1　Maintains Self-Control	.1　Responds calmly—feels strong emotions, such as anger or extreme frustration, but controls these emotions and calmly continues discussions or other processes.
	.2　Uses stress-management techniques to ontrol response, prevent burnout, and deal with ongoing stress, thus managing stress effectively.
B.6.2 COMPETENCY CLUSTER: Self-Confidence Self-Confidence is a person's belief in one's own capability to accomplish a task. This includes a person expressing confidence in dealing with increasingly challenging circumstances, in reaching decisions or forming opinions, and in handling failures constructively.	
Element	**Performance Criteria**
B.6.2.1　Creates an Environment of Confidence	.1　Sees self as competent, comparing oneself or one's own abilities favorably with others and their abilities.
	.2　Sees self as causal agent, prime mover, catalyst, or originator, stating confidence in one's own judgment.
	.3　Develops an element of trust and confidentiality.
B.6.2.2　Accepts Failure Positively	.1　Accepts responsibility; admits failures or shortcomings in a specific, non-global manner—"I misjudged the situation."
	.2　Learns from own mistakes, analyzing own performance to understand failures and to improve future performance.
B.6.3 COMPETENCY CLUSTER: Flexibility Flexibility is the ability to adapt to and work effectively with a variety of situations, individuals, or groups. It is the ability to understand and appreciate different and opposing perspectives on an issue, to adapt an approach as the requirements of a situation change, and to change or easily accept changes in one's own organization or job requirements.	
Element	**Performance Criteria**
B.6.3.1　Changes to Meet the Needs of the Project	.1　Flexibly applies rules or procedures, depending on the individual situation. Adapts actions to accomplish organization's larger objectives.
	.2　Adapts tactics to situation or to other's response, changing own behavior or approach to suit the situation.
	.3　Respects personal, ethnic, and cultural differences in order to ensure a collaborative project environment.
B.6.3.2　Changes at the Required Pace	.1　Changes quickly when necessary.
B.6.4 COMPETENCY CLUSTER: Organizational Commitment Organizational Commitment is the individual's ability and willingness to align one's own behavior with the needs, priorities, and goals of the organization, to act in ways that promote organizational goals or meet organizational needs.	
Element	**Performance Criteria**
B.6.4.1　Demonstrates Commitment to the Project	.1　Understands and actively supports project and organization mission and goals.
	.2　Aligns own activities and priorities to meet organizational needs; understands need for cooperation to achieve larger organizational objectives.
	.3　Makes sacrifices when necessary to move project forward.

Table 3-6. Personal Effectiveness Unit of Competence

Section 4

Developing Competence as a Project Manager

Introduction

The first stage in developing competence, in any field, is to determine one's relative ranking against the performance criteria describing competence. The performance criteria in the *PMCD Framework* were developed to apply generically to all project managers regardless of the nature, type, size, or complexity of projects in which they are engaged. In other words, the *PMCD Framework* was developed to apply to project managers leading most projects most of the time. It defines the criteria for a project manager to be deemed competent across all nine (9) Knowledge Areas and five (5) Project Management Processes defined in the *PMBOK® Guide*. The generic nature of the *PMCD Framework* is necessary to ensure that both:
- Project management competence in individuals is transferable across industries
- Industries and organizations are able to utilize the *PMCD Framework* as a basis for the development of more industry- and organization-specific competency models.

The generic nature of the *PMCD Framework* is underpinned by its use of the *PMBOK® Guide,* PMI's *Project Management Experience and Knowledge Self-Assessment Manual*, and PMI's *Project Management Professional (PMP) Role Delineation Study* as primary references. To this end, the *PMCD Framework* outlines the knowledge, demonstrable performance, and personal requirements for a project manager to be deemed as competent in leading and/or managing most projects most of the time.

Tailoring Assessments

As part of their process for using the *PMCD Framework* in tailoring their own assessments, organizations and project managers would have to determine the overall relevance of the discrete elements and performance criteria. Thus, if there were elements and performance criteria that did not apply to their situations, these could be left out of their assessment in order to tailor the instrument to better align with their line of business or organization. Tailoring could also include items such as identifying the relative importance of different competencies. However, individuals and organizations must exercise judgment in applying the *PMCD Framework* for defining project manager competence within their environment. Those constructing these instruments should keep in mind that the *PMCD Framework* was developed to describe competence in project managers needed in leading most projects most of the time. The generic nature of the *PMCD Framework* was deliberately constructed to ensure that project manager competence in individuals would be transferable across organizations and industries. Arbitrarily omitting any elements or performance criteria from an assessment instrument means that the individuals and/or organizations being assessed will not receive any feedback as to their level of competence regarding these criteria.

Another shortfall associated with a selective approach in applying the *PMCD Framework* would be to set up a situation where different project managers and organizations would effectively create their own definitions of project manager competence. This undermines the transferability construct contained within the *PMCD Framework*. Project managers and organizations should exercise sound judgment when deciding to eliminate certain elements or performance criteria from their assessments—especially if one of their goals is to establish a uniform standard for determining project manager competence. If certain elements and/or performance criteria are not applicable within their operating environment, the organization must decide whether to include these when applying the *PMCD Framework*. In order to promote a wider transferability across industry, the organization may choose to keep these items and develop these competencies within their project managers.

Methodology for Achieving Competence

A suggested methodology for achieving competence as a project manager in each of the three separate dimensions of competence, as outlined within the *PMCD Framework* (Project Management Knowledge, Project Management Performance, and Personal Competency), progresses through five stages:
• Stage 1: Determine Applicable Elements and Performance Criteria
• Stage 2: Determine Desired Levels of Proficiency
• Stage 3: Assessment
• Stage 4: Addressing Gaps in Competence
• Stage 5: Progression Toward Competence.

Stage 1: Determine Applicable Elements and Performance Criteria

The first stage of the methodology requires that the individual or organization determine which elements and performance criteria contained within the *PMCD Framework* are applicable within the environment that their project managers work. By selecting applicable items, they are, in effect, creating a customized framework designed for the environment in which they run their projects. There is a natural conflict contained within this activity. First, there is the need to limit the elements and performance criteria to those that are relevant to the environment where their project managers execute their work. Secondly, there is the need to retain a broad enough context for their customized framework such that they do not overly restrict the applicability of the competencies being sought for their project managers. It is only through the application of sound judgment that a customized framework can be selected that both 1) limits the scope of the elements and performance criteria to those applicable to the current environment, and 2) still provides sufficient breadth that it is transferable across the potential environments where the project manager may practice.

When selecting the appropriate elements and performance criteria, a related activity addresses the question of which items are appropriate for a given level of project manager. Many organizations develop their project managers by systematically assigning them to projects of increasing complexity. This approach progressively builds the competence of their project managers as they tackle the training and experience needed to run increasingly more complex projects. For example, a new project manager would be trained and assigned to simple projects of relatively short duration requiring limited interaction across functional groups or groups of clients. As the competence level of the project manager increases, the focus on development shifts toward developing competencies related to managing more complex projects, cutting across multidiscipline groups. The approach continues until the focus is on building the competency of the highest level of project manager within the organization.

One approach to help accomplish this activity is through the use of interviews with qualified project managers. The individual or organization can solicit input from successful project managers who are deemed as being "competent" by their organization. The input will help to select the set of elements and performance criteria that is viewed as being relevant to success within their environment. Another approach collects input from managers who manage project managers. Both approaches seek to determine the collective opinion as to which items from the *PMCD Framework* are applicable for the particular environment in which the project managers will be executing their role.

Stage 2: Determine Desired Levels of Proficiency

The next stage in the methodology looks to determine what the desired level of proficiency is for each of the performance criteria selected from the *PMCD Framework*. For example, is the desired level of proficiency that of being able to exhibit the competency across all situations as described? Or, is it desired that the individual be knowledgeable of the competency being addressed, yet not fully proficient to the degree that they can execute the competency without help? Only the individual or organization applying the *PMCD Framework* can answer these questions.

Again, this stage has a natural conflict within its execution. Sound judgment must be applied in order to create a profile of elements and performance criteria. The appropriate desired levels of proficiency should match the environment within which the project manager will execute projects—while at the same time maintaining a sufficient breadth to allow the development of project manager competence providing transportability across organizations.

Stage 3: Assessment

The third stage of the methodology is primarily assessment by organizations or individual project managers to ascertain their strengths and weaknesses against the elements and performance criteria selected from Sections 2 and 3 of the *PMCD Framework*. For **Project Management Knowledge Competencies,** assessment would address areas of underpinning knowledge and understanding of project management (i.e., "what they know about what is to be done" and "why they have to do it").

For **Project Management Performance Competencies,** assessment would address individual project managers' abilities to perform a project-related activity (i.e., "what they are able to do or accomplish while applying their project management knowledge").

For **Personal Competencies,** assessment would address areas of project manager behavior (i.e., "how they behave when performing the project or activity").

For individuals, this process helps to identify any deficiencies or "gaps" in competence. From this, a strategy outlining the methods to be pursued to address gaps, or to enhance areas of competence that are considered to be not as strong as others, needs to be developed. Organizations are also able to use the process of assessment to map the strengths and weaknesses in competence in their workforce and to develop the necessary strategies to address any gaps discovered.

Stage 4: Addressing Gaps in Competence

Once gaps in individual competence are identified, they should be addressed in order to enhance competence in that specific area. However, the processes for addressing such gaps differ for each dimension of competence. Reassessment must occur after action is taken to address the gaps to determine whether further action is needed.

Project Management Knowledge Competencies: Individuals are able to address gaps in their underpinning knowledge and understanding by a variety of measures, including:
- Attendance at training and education programs
- Gaining relevant project experience in the workplace, either directly or by related means
- Networking with other project managers through professional industry or organizational agencies.

Project Management Performance Competencies: Gaps in the area of performance competencies are usually addressed through participation in performance measurement and appraisal programs, additional experience gained while working in project environments or through participation in recognized programs conducted by professional industry and organizational agencies. As the project manager gains experience in managing projects, he should be better able to provide evidence of demonstrable performance against the performance criteria for this dimension of competence.

Project Management Personal Competencies: Individuals are able to address gaps in their underpinning knowledge and understanding of a given behavioral competency area by a variety of measures. These measures may include:
- Attendance at training and education programs aimed at gaining a better understanding about human behavior and motivation

- Gaining relevant project experience in the workplace, either directly or by related means
- Networking with other project managers through professional industry or organizational agencies
- Working with a mentor who can help project managers better assess themselves within this competency dimension
- Exposure to peer and/or management reviews and feedback.

The "gaps" identified in any elements or performance criteria can also serve as valuable input in constructing the objectives of project manager training sessions or developmental activities. This allows construction of employee development programs targeted to those specific areas and, thus, helps to conserve funds available for employee development.

Stage 5: Progression Toward Competence

By progressively addressing identified gaps in their competence, individual project managers are able to achieve competence in each Unit of each Dimension included in their specified assessment.

Realization of competence in Project Management Knowledge and Project Management Performance cannot be achieved for individual Units only—i.e., an individual cannot be deemed completely competent as a project manager by being deemed competent in Risk Management only.

Attainment of competence in the Personal Competencies is much more difficult, since it deals with personality traits, motivators, and drivers. Therefore, the goal should be to continuously improve in these competency areas. In order for a project manager to be judged completely competent in this dimension, he must demonstrate the desired behaviors defined by the *PMCD Framework* while working in a project management environment.

Fulfillment of competence is also affected by the individual's or organization's selection of elements and performance criteria in applying the *PMCD Framework*. If they have been overly restrictive and have narrowly selected criteria that only apply to their environment or situation, then their competence will only relate to that environment. If they have selected a broader range of elements and performance criteria, then their competence will apply more broadly across different organizations and environments. The more broadly they adhere to the *PMCD Framework,* the more transportable their competence as project managers.

Project Manager Competency Summary Scorecard

The *PMCD Framework* includes an example of a Summary Scorecard. This scorecard can be used to document the project manager's overall assessment results of one's competency levels in each of the Units of Competence described in the *PMCD Framework*. The Summary Scorecard has suggested rating scales that allow a project manager to better describe the level of competence as one goes through an assessment process. As part of the assessment process, the project manager should use these scales to self-rate against the performance criteria defined within the *PMCD Framework*. After rating oneself against the performance criteria, the project manager can transfer personal average scores for each Unit of Competence within each Dimension to the Summary Scorecard. This approach allows a project manager to obtain a composite view of one's overall level of competence as a project manager. The ultimate goal as a project manager would be to build an overall competence level so that one would be able to score at the top of the scale in each area.

Organizations can also use the scorecard to document the relative strength of the project managers within the organization against the competencies defined within the *PMCD Framework*. Using this approach allows the organization to focus on building those areas of competence where its project managers do not rank at the levels desired by the organization.

Project Manager Competency Summary Scorecard

Project Manager: _____   Assessment Date: _____   Assessor: _____

PM Knowledge & Performance Competencies

Component	Initiation		Planning		Execution		Controlling		Closing	
(PMBOK® Knowledge Areas)	Knowledge	Performance	Knowledge	Performance	Knowledge	Performance	Knowledge	Performance	Knowledge	Performance
Project Integration Management										
Project Scope Management										
Project Time Management										
Project Cost Management										
Project Quality Management										
Project Human Resources Management										
Project Communications Management										
Project Risk Management										
Project Procurement Management										
# areas with no gaps										
# areas with marginal gaps										
# areas with significant gaps										

Rating Scales

Score	PM Knowledge Competencies (Knowledge & Understanding)
0	Not Rated
1	Exposed to Concepts - Familiar with terms and concepts.
2	Development Needed - Exhibits a limited level of the knowledge and understanding expected.
3	Proficient - Exhibits an acceptable level of knowledge and understanding of this area.

Score	PM Performance Competencies (Demonstrable Performance)
0	Not Rated
1	Has not had opportunity to demonstrate one or more attributes of this competency.
2	Has not fully demonstrated this competency as described.
3	Has fully demonstrated this competency as described.

Score	Personal Competencies (Behaviors and Motivators)
0	Not Rated
1	Minimally Effective - Barely exhibits this competency the way we expect of PMs.
2	Effective - Exhibits an adequate example of this competency across most situations.
3	Highly Effective - Exhibits a very good example of this competency across all situations.

Comments:

Personal Competencies

Traits	Score
Achievement and Action	
Achievement Orientation	
Concern for Order, Quality, and Accuracy	
Initiative	
Information Seeking	
Helping and Human Service	
Customer Service Orientation	
Interpersonal Understanding	
Impact and Influence	
Impact and Influence	
Organizational Awareness	
Relationship Building	
Managerial	
Teamwork and Cooperation	
Developing Others	
Team Leadership	
Directiveness: Assertiveness and Use of Positional Power	
Cognitive	
Analytical Thinking	
Conceptual Thinking	
Personal Effectiveness	
Self-Control	
Self-Confidence	
Flexibility	
Organizational Commitment	
# areas with no gaps	
# areas with marginal gaps	
# areas with significant gaps	

Figure 4-1. Project Manager Competency Scorecard

Appendix A

The Project Management Institute (PMI) Standards-Setting Process

The Project Management Institute (PMI) Standards-Setting Process was established initially as Institute policy by a vote of the PMI Board of Directors at its October 1993 meeting. In March 1998, the PMI Board of Directors approved modifications to the process. Then, in March 1999, it was modified again to make it consistent with the concurrent change in PMI governance procedures.

A.1 PMI STANDARDS DOCUMENTS

PMI Standards Documents are those developed or published by PMI that describe generally accepted practices of project management, specifically:
- *A Guide to the Project Management Body of Knowledge (PMBOK® Guide)*
- Project Management Body of Knowledge handbooks.

Additional documents may be added to this list by the PMI Standards Manager, subject to the advice and consent of the PMI Project Management Standards Program Member Advisory Group and the PMI Chief Executive Officer. Standards Documents may be original works published by PMI, or they may be publications by other organizations or individuals.

Standards Documents will be developed in accordance with the Code of Good Practice for Standardization developed by the International Organization for Standardization (ISO) and the standards development guidelines established by the American National Standards Institute (ANSI).

A.2 DEVELOPMENT OF ORIGINAL WORKS

Standards Documents that are original works developed by PMI, or revisions of such documents, will be handled as follows:
- Prospective developer(s) will submit a proposal to the PMI Standards Manager. The Manager may also request such proposals. The Manager will submit all received proposals to the PMI Standards Program Member Advisory Group who, with the Manager, will decide whether to accept or reject each proposal.
- The Manager will inform the prospective developer(s) as to the decision and the rationale for the decision. If an approved proposal requires funding in excess of that budgeted for standards development, the Manager will submit the proposal to the PMI Chief Executive Officer for funding.
- For all approved and funded proposals, the Manager will support the developer's efforts so as to maximize the probability that the end product will be accepted. Developer(s) will be required to sign the PMI Volunteer Assignment of Copyright.

• When the proposed material has been completed to the satisfaction of the developer(s), the developer(s) will submit the material to the PMI Standards Manager. The PMI Standards Program Member Advisory Group, with the Manager, will review the proposed material and decide whether to initiate further review by knowledgeable individuals or request additional work by the developer(s).

• The Manager will appoint, subject to review and approval by the PMI Standards Program Member Advisory Group, at least three knowledgeable individuals to review and comment on the material. Based on comments received, the Member Advisory Group will decide whether to accept the material as an exposure draft.

• The PMI Standards Manager will develop a plan for obtaining appropriate public review for each exposure draft. The plan will include a) a review period of not less than one month and not more than six months, b) announcement in *PMI Today* (and/or any other similarly appropriate media) of the availibility of the exposure draft for review, and c) cost of review copies. The PMI Standards Program Member Advisory Group must approve the Manager's plan for public review. Each exposure draft will include a notice asking for comments to be sent to the PMI Standards Manager at PMI Headquarters, and noting the length of, and expiration date for, the review period.

• Exposure drafts will be published under the aegis of the PMI Publishing Department and must meet the standards of that group regarding typography and style.

• During the review period, the Manager will solicit formal input of the Managers of other PMI Programs (e.g., Certification, Education, Components, and Publishing) that may be affected by the future publication of the material as a PMI Standard.

• At the conclusion of the review period, the PMI Standards Manager will review comments received with the PMI Standards Program Member Advisory Group, and will work with the developer(s) and others as needed to incorporate appropriate comments. If the comments are major, the PMI Standards Program Member Advisory Group may elect to repeat the exposure draft review process.

• When the PMI Standards Manager and the PMI Standards Program Member Advisory Group have approved a proposed PMI Standards Document, the Manager will promptly submit the document to the PMI Chief Executive Officer for final review and approval. The PMI Chief Executive Officer will verify compliance with procedures and ensure that member input was sufficient. The PMI Chief Executive Officer will a) approve the document as submitted; b) reject the document; or c) request additional review, and will provide explanatory comments in support of the chosen option.

A.3 ADOPTION OF NON-ORIGINAL WORKS AS STANDARDS

Standards Documents that are the work of other organizations or individuals will be handled as follows:

• Any person or organization may submit a request to the PMI Standards Manager to consider a non-PMI publication as a PMI Standard. The Manager will submit all proposals received to the PMI Standards Program Member Advisory Group who, with the Manager, will decide whether to accept or reject each proposal. If accepted, the Manager will appoint, subject to review and approval by the PMI Standards Program Member Advisory Group, at least three knowledgeable individuals to review and comment on the material.

• During the review period, the Manager will solicit the formal input of the Managers of other PMI Programs (e.g., Certification, Education, Components, and Publishing) that may be affected by the future publication of the material as a PMI Standard.

• Based on comments received, the Member Advisory Group, with the Manager, will decide whether to a) accept the proposal as written as a PMI Standard, b) accept the proposal with modifications and/or an addendum as a PMI Standard, c) seek further review and comment on the proposal (that is, additional reviewers and/or issuance as an exposure draft), or d) reject the proposal. The Manager will inform the submitter as to the decision and the rationale for the decision.

• When the PMI Standards Manager and the PMI Standards Program Member Advisory Group have approved a proposed PMI Standards Document, the Manager will promptly submit the document to the PMI Chief Executive Officer for final review and approval. The Manager will prepare a proposal for the PMI Chief Executive Officer for consideration of a prospective relationship with the owner(s) of the material.

• The PMI Chief Executive Officer will verify compliance with procedures and will ensure that member input was sufficient. The PMI Chief Executive Officer will a) approve the document as submitted; b) reject the document; or c) request additional review, and will provide explanatory comments in support of the chosen option.

Appendix B

Evolution of the PMCD Framework

The Project Management Institute (PMI®) sponsored the Project Management Competency (PMC) project starting in 1998 to work on a competency framework for project managers. The purpose of the project was to develop a Project Manager Competency Development (PMCD) Framework that described the competencies likely to lead to effective project manager performance across various contexts. The competency framework was to be for use in *professional development* of project managers rather than for use in selection or performance evaluation.

Justification for the project came from PMI's recognition that, increasingly, both public and private-sector organizations were realizing that good project management is necessary to their future success, and that good project management requires competent project managers. In order to help address this need, a variety of organizations have developed competency frameworks. These frameworks generally fall into one of two categories:

1. They are organization- or application-area-specific and thus, while adequate for their defined purpose, do not appear to meet the needs of the profession as a whole.
2. They are assessment- or evaluation-oriented and again, while they may be adequate for their defined purpose, do not address the need for development-oriented guidance.

PMI recognizes that professionalism in project management is greatly facilitated by a project management competency framework that:
- Is generally accepted throughout the profession
- Provides guidance to both individuals and organizations regarding how to manage the professional growth of a project manager
- Addresses a full range of project types from small and simple to large and complex.

Consequently, in late 1998, PMI asked for volunteers to develop a *standard* outlining a PMCD Framework and sponsored the PMC project team. Janet Szumal was selected as the project manager for the PMC project team, taking over from Bill Duncan, who had been serving as the team lead when the project's scope was being defined. The *PMCD Framework* was to identify and define some of the key dimensions of effective performance, the competencies that likely impact performance, and the contingencies likely to influence the extent to which a particular competency had an impact on project manager performance. A volunteer team was assembled and, during the course of the next year, worked on refining the project's scope, reviewing the literature, and starting to develop the basic framework and definitions outlining project manager competency.

In late summer 1999, Szumal had to relinquish her role as volunteer PMC project manager due to conflicting time commitments, and the project team disbanded. PMI sought a new volunteer project manager to lead the PMC project and in November 1999, Scott Gill, PMP, was approved as the new *PMCD Framework* Standard project manager. Immediate efforts began to assemble a new team of volunteers to carry on the project. Dave Violette, PMP, was named as Deputy Project Manager, and the PMC project was re-launched in March 2000 with a new group of volunteer team members. The new team immediately began the job of building upon the work of the previous team. A core team of subject-matter experts was assembled from the volunteer team members. Core team members were chosen based upon their experience in managing projects, surveying techniques, or developing competency models to guide the professional development of others. The core team reviewed applicable references and the collective input from the balance of the PMC team. As work progressed, several revisions of the draft *PMCD Framework* were submitted to the entire project team for its review and comment, with the team's collective input being used to revise the overall *PMCD Framework*. During this stage, the project team adopted the elements of competence and performance criteria published in the National Competency Standards for Project Management prepared by the Australian Institute of Project Management (AIPM).

In the fall of 2000, PMI published the *Project Management Professional (PMP) Role Delineation Study* and the *Project Management Experience and Knowledge Self-Assessment Manual*. The PMC core team reviewed this work in comparison to the elements and criteria contained in the draft *PMCD Framework*. A decision was made to revise the elements of competence and performance criteria contained within the *PMCD Framework* to align with the *Project Management Professional (PMP) Role Delineation Study* and the *Project Management Experience and Knowledge Self-Assessment Manual*. The PMC core team, with support from the PMI Project Management Standards Program, conducted a Standards "Open Working Session" at PMI 2000 in Houston, Texas, USA. Additional input was solicited from those attending the session regarding the completeness and usefulness of the draft *PMCD Framework*. Input indicated that the draft *PMCD Framework* would serve as a useful resource for those working to develop the competence of project managers within their organizations.

Following the aforementioned "Open Working Session," and based upon guidance from PMI, the PMC project team revised the original scope of the project to eliminate the phase designed to incorporate assorted contingency variables into the *PMCD Framework*. The project scope was revised to apply generically to all project managers regardless of the nature, type, size, or complexity of the projects in which they are engaged. The *PMCD Framework* was revised to apply to project managers leading most projects most of the time. The project's scope was further revised to eliminate a further content-validation phase that had originally been planned to follow the identification of contingency variables affecting project manager competence. The decision to eliminate a separate validation phase was based on the fact that the approach used in developing the *PMCD Framework* assured that it had content validity (it was built on previous research and used an expert panel to identify the specifics of the framework), plus the fact that its content validity would be further tested by comments to the exposure draft (described in the *PMBOK® Guide*).

Following these changes in project scope, the *PMCD Framework* went through another round of revisions to prepare it for exposure draft. Following these revisions, several extensive rounds of review by the entire PMC project team were conducted to ensure that the newly revised *PMCD Framework* still held valid content.

The resultant draft of the *PMCD Framework* was submitted to PMI in March 2001 for consideration as an exposure draft to be circulated among PMI membership and other affected parties. The proposed exposure draft was submitted for formal review to six subject-matter experts. The *PMCD Framework* project team evaluated the comments from these six reviewers and the Standards Member Advisory Group. A final draft was submitted to PMI and approved for this exposure draft.

The exposure draft was submitted for public review on 1 October 2001 and closed on 3 December 2001. During this period 154 comments/recommendations were received. Each one was evaluated, and decisions were made as to whether or not to incorporate them into this document.

Appendix C

Contributors and Reviewers

Current PMCD Framework Project Team

Core Team Members

Scott Gill, MBA, PMP – PMCD Framework Standard Project Manager
David Violette, MBA, PMP – PMCD Framework Standard Deputy Project Manager
William C. (Clifton) Baldwin, MS
Christophe Bredillet, D.Sc., MBA
Chris Cartwright, PMP
Paul Fiala, MS
Kenneth J. Stevenson, MS

Review Team Members

Sumner Alpert, MBA, PMP
Dennis Bolles, PMP
Craig Garvin, PMP
Gilbert Guay
Hans Jonasson, PMP
Jacob Stranger Kgamphe
Barbara Marino, MPM, PMP
Kevin Porter, PMP
Angela Sheets
Shoukat M. Sheikh, MBA, PMP
Alberto Villa, MBA, PMP
Thomas Williamson, PMP
Xiaolan Wang

Initial PMCD Framework Project Team

Janet Szumal, Ph.D. – PMCD Framework Standard Project Manager
Nicola Barron
Christophe Bredillet, D.Sc., MBA
Chris Cartwright, PMP

John Chiorini, Ph.D., PMP
Rob Cooke, Ph.D.
Lynn Crawford
Russ Darnell, MS
David Denny, PMP
Karen DiPierro
Kathleen Donohue, PMP
Dick Drews, PMP
Ellen Edman
David Garbitt
Larry Goldsmith, PMP
William C. Grigg, PE, PMP
Brad King
Alan Kristynik, PMP
Rose Mary Lewis, PMP
Lawrence Mack, PE, PMP
Barbara Marino, MPM, PMP
Dave Maynard, MBA, PMP
Vrinda Menon, PMP
Richard Ray
Paul Rust, PMP
Philip Sharpe, PMP
Gregory Skulmoski
Cyndi Snyder, PMP
Ken Stevenson, MS
Dick Waltz, PMP
Greg Willits, PMP
Peter Wynne
Frank Yanagimachi

Selected Reviewers of Pre-Exposure Draft

These volunteers provided specific evaluations and comments on the pre-exposure draft. The project team and the PMI Standards Program Team considered their input in the development of the exposure draft.
James P. Henderson, Ph.D.
Normand Pettersen, Ph.D.
Lynn Crawford
Tomas Linhard
T.I. Morris

Reviewers of Exposure Draft

Kim Colenso, PMP
Judy VanMeter
Nigel Blampied
Portia Saul, PMP
Crispin Piney, PMP
Brian Hobbs, PMP
Cyndi Snyder, PMP
Jody A. McIlrath

Greg Skulmoski
George Sukumar, PE

PMI Standards Program Member Advisory Group 2001-2002

Sergio R. Coronado, Spain
J. Brian Hobbs, PMP, Canada
Tom Kurihara, USA
Bobbye S. Underwood, PMP, USA
Julia M. Bednar, PMP, USA
George Belev, USA
Cynthia A. Berg, PMP, USA

PMI Headquarters Staff

Steven L. Fahrenkrog, PMP, Standards Manager
Kristin L. Wright, Standards Program Administrator
Iesha Brown, Certification Program Administrator
Eva Goldman, Technical Research Standards Associate
Linda Cherry, Publisher
Richard Schwartz, Book Development Editor
Danielle Moore, Book Publishing Planner

Project Management Competency Glossary

This glossary includes terms that are used in the *PMCD Framework*. These terms are not unique to project manager competence, but may be used differently or with a narrower meaning than that of general everyday usage.

Ability: The quality of being able to do something; the physical, mental, financial, or legal power to perform; a natural or acquired skill or talent.

Attitudes: Relatively lasting feelings, beliefs, and behavior tendencies directed toward specific persons, groups, ideas, issues, or objects. They are often described in terms of three components: 1) an affective component, or the feelings, sentiments, moods, and emotions about some person, idea, event, or object; 2) a cognitive component, or the beliefs, opinions, knowledge, or information held by the individual; and, 3) a behavioral component, or the intention and predisposition to act.

Behavior: The manner in which an individual acts or conducts oneself under specified circumstances.

Competency: A cluster of related knowledge, attitudes, skills, and other personal characteristics that affects a major part of one's job (i.e., one or more key roles or responsibilities), correlates with performance on the job, can be measured against well-accepted standards, and can be improved via training and development.

Major components of competencies include:
- Abilities
- Attitudes
- Behavior
- Knowledge
- Personality
- Skills.

Major dimensions of competency include:

PM Knowledge Competency: The knowledge and understanding that a project manager brings to a project. This can include qualifications and experience, both direct and related. These are the knowledge components of competence.

Personal Competency: The core personality characteristics underlying a person's capability to do a project. These are the behavior, motives, traits, attitudes, and self-concepts that enable a person to successfully manage a project.

PM Performance Competency: The ability to perform the activities within an occupational area to the levels of performance expected in employment. This competency dimension looks at the demonstrable performance of the individual in executing project management tasks.

Competency Cluster: See **Competency.**

Competency Dictionary: A general comprehensive list of the competencies that are included in the competency framework for a job, usually grouped by clusters.

Competency Dimensions: A multidimensional framework that breaks competency into dimensions of knowledge, performance and personal competence.

Competency Gap: The difference between the desired level of competence within a given dimension and the level of competence assessed for an individual. It is the "gaps" in one's competence that an individual aims to improve through individual development.

Effective Performance: An intended or expected accomplishment.

Elements of Competence: The basic building blocks of the Unit of Competence. They describe, in output terms, actions or outcomes, which are demonstrable and assessable.

Intent: The motive or trait force that is the basis which may result in, or cause action toward, an outcome.

Knowledge: A body of information (conceptual, factual, procedural) that can be directly applied to the performance of tasks.

Motives: Things a person consistently thinks about or wants that cause action. Motives "drive and select" behavior toward certain action or goals and away from others.

Performance Criteria: Refers to an integrated list of aspects of performance that would be regarded as displaying competent performance in the workplace in an Element of Competency.

Personality: A unique organization of a relatively stable set of characteristics, tendencies, and temperaments that define an individual and determine that person's interaction with the environment.

Project Performance: A measure of the extent to which the project is carried out as planned in terms of objectives, time, and financial constraints, and organizational policies and procedures.

Project Success: For the purpose of this document, project success is defined as a collective assessment by project stakeholders (e.g., client/customer, sponsor) of the degree to which the project has achieved each of its objectives.

Self-Concept: View of oneself, often different than the view others hold of the individual.

Skill: Proficiency, facility, or dexterity that is acquired or developed through training or experience; an art, trade or technique, requiring the use of the hands, body, or mind.

Style: A set of skills, attributes, or characteristics of a person; the concept refers to a frequent pattern of what is said, done, expressed, or performed by a person demonstrating one's values. It encompasses the modes or patterns of behavior that people exhibit in approaching their work and interacting with others.

Subject-Matter Expert: A person, usually an accomplished performer, who knows the knowledge, performance, and personal competence required for a given Unit or Cluster of Competence.

Trait: A distinguishing feature of the person's character, usually thought of as a relatively enduring aspect of the person.

Unit of Competence: A major segment of overall Competency, typically representing a major function.

©2002 Project Management Institute, Four Campus Boulevard, Newtown Square, PA 19073-3299 USA

References

The American Heritage Dictionary of the English Language, 3rd ed. 1992. Houghton Mifflin.

Australian Institute of Project Management (AIPM). 1996. *National Competency Standards for Project Management*. Split Junction, NSW.

Boyatzis, Richard E. 1982. *The competent manager: A model for effective performance*. New York: John Wiley & Sons.

Crawford, L.H. 1997. A global approach to project management competence. *Proceedings of the 1997 AIPM National Conference, Gold Coast*, Brisbane: AIPM: 220–228.

——. 1998. Project management competence for strategy realization. *Proceedings of the 14th World Congress on Project Management*. Ljubljana, Slovenia 1: 10–21.

——. 1999. Assessing and developing project management competence. *Proceedings of the 30th Annual Project Management Institute 1999 Seminars & Symposium*. Newtown Square, PA: Project Management Institute.

Finn, R. 1993. A synthesis of current research on management competencies. Working Paper HWP9310. Henley-on-Thames, Henley Management College.

Gonczi, A., P. Hager, et al. 1993. *The development of competency-based assessment strategies for the professions*. Canberra: Australian Government Publishing Service.

Hellriegel, Don, John W. Slocum Jr., and Richard W. Woodman. 1992. *Organizational behavior*. 6th ed. St. Paul: West.

Heneman, Herbert G. III, and Robert L. Heneman. 1994. *Staffing organizations*. Middleton: Mendota House.

Heywood, L., A. Gonczi, et al. 1992. *A guide to development of competency standards for professionals*. Canberra: Australian Government Publishing Service.

Kleinmuntz, Benjamin. 1985. *Personality and psychological assessment*. Malabar: Robert E. Krieger.

Mealiea, Laird W., and Gary P. Latham. 1996. *Skills for managerial success: Theory, experience, and practice*. Chicago: Irwin.

Parry, Scott B. 1998. Just what is a competency? (And why should you care?) *Training* (June): 58–64.

Project Management Institute. 2000. *A guide to the project management body of knowledge (PMBOK guide) - 2000 edition*. Newtown Square, PA: Project Management Institute.

——. 2000. *Project management experience and knowledge self-assessment manual*. Newtown Square, PA: Project Management Institute.

Spencer, Lyle M., Jr., and Signe M. Spencer. 1993. *Competence at work: Models for superior performance*. New York: John Wiley & Sons.

Additional References

Aguinis, Herman, and Kurt Kraiger. 1997. Practicing what we preach: Competency-based assessment of industrial/organizational psychology graduate students. *The Industrial-Organizational Psychologist* (April): 34–39.

Anastasi, Anne. 1988. *Psychological testing.* 6th ed. New York: Macmillan.

Bacharach, Samuel B. 1989. Organizational theories: Some criteria for evaluation. *Academy of Management Review* 14 (4): 496–515.

Belout, Adnane. 1997. Effects of human resource management on project effectiveness and success: Toward a new conceptual framework. *International Journal of Project Management* 16 (1): 21–26.

Cascio, Wayne F. 1992. *Managing human resources: Productivity, quality of work life, Profits.* 3rd ed. New York: McGraw-Hill.

Dale, Margaret, and Paul Iles. 1992. *Assessing management skills: A guide to competencies and evaluation techniques.* London: Kogan.

Gadeken, Owen C. 1997. Project managers as leaders: Competencies of top performers. *Army RD&A Magazine* (January-February): 2–7.

McLagan, Patricia A. 1997. Competencies: The next generation. *Training & Development* 51 (May): 40–47.

McClelland, David C. 1973. Testing for competence rather than for "intelligence." *American Psychologist* (January): 1–14.

McVeigh, Bryan J. 1995. The right stuff revisited: A competency perspective of Army program managers. *Program Manager* (January-February): 30–34.

Mealiea, Laird W., and Gary P. Latham. 1996. *Skills for managerial success: Theory, experience, and practice.* Chicago, IL: Irwin.

Messick, Samuel. 1980. Test validity and the ethics of assessment. *American Psychologist* 35 (11): 1012–1027.

Mirabile, Richard J. 1997. Everything you wanted to know about competency modeling. *Training & Development* 51 (8): 73–77.

Morris, P.W.G. 1999. Body Building. Paper presented on project management forum (www.pmforum.org/digest/newapr99.htm).

Pinto, J.K., and Slevin, D.P. 1988. Project success: Definitions and measurement techniques. *Journal of Project Management* 19 (1): 67–72.

Posner, Barry Z. 1987. What it takes to be a good project manager. *Project Management Journal* (March).

Project Management Institute. 2000. *Project management professional (PMP) role delineation study.* Newtown Square, PA: Project Management Institute.

Skulmoski, Greg. 1999. New locks and keys: Is cost engineering ready to contribute? *Presented at 43rd Annual Meeting of AACE International* (June).

Struckenbruck, L.C. 1986. Who determines project success? *PMI Seminar/Symposium Proceedings:* 85–93.

Thamhain, H.J., and Wilemon, D.L. 1982. Developing project/program managers. *PMI Seminar/Symposium Proceedings,* II-B.1–II-B.10.

Toney, Frank. 1998. The quest to find the superior project manager: The fortune 500 project management benchmarking forum defines competencies. *PM Network* (July).

Ulrich, D., Brockbank, W., Yeung, A.K., and Lake, D.G. 1995. Human resource competencies: An empirical assessment. *Human Resource Management* 34 (4): 473–495.

Waller, Ron. 1997. A project manager competency model. *Proceedings of the 28th Annual Project Management Institute 1997 Seminars & Symposium.* Newtown Square, PA: Project Management.

Online References

The Association for Project Management. "The 40 Key Competencies" (http://www.apmgroup.co.uk/apmbok.htm).

NASA. "Academy of Program/Project Leadership" (formally called "NASA's Program/Project Management Initiative") (http://www.msfc.nasa.gov/training/PPMI/HOME.html).

"Project performance measurement standards." (http://www.acq.osd.mil/pm/internat/ppms.htm).

Treasury Board of Canada Secretariat. "An Enhanced Framework for the Management of Information Technology Projects–Project Management Core Competencies" (http://www.cio-dpi.gc.ca/efit/english/Solutions/cc/PMCCE.html).

Index

©2002 Project Management Institute, Four Campus Boulevard, Newtown Square, PA 19073-3299 USA

Upgrade Your Project Management Knowledge with Leading Titles from PMI

A Guide to the Project Management Body of Knowledge (PMBOK® Guide) – 2000 Edition

Project Management Institute

The Project Management Institute's (PMI®) PMBOK® Guide has become the essential sourcebook for the project management profession and its de facto global standard, with over 900,000 copies in circulation worldwide. It has been designated an American National Standard by the American National Standards Institute (ANSI) and is one of the major references used by candidates to study for the Project Management Professional (PMP®) Certification Examination. This new edition incorporates numerous recommendations and changes to the 1996 edition, including: progressive elaboration is given more emphasis; the role of the project office is acknowledged; the treatment of earned value is expanded in three chapters; the linkage between organizational strategy and project management is strengthened throughout; and the chapter on risk management has been rewritten with six processes instead of four. Newly added processes, tools, and techniques are aligned with the five project management processes and nine knowledge areas.

ISBN: 1-880410-23-0 (paperback)
ISBN: 1-880410-22-2 (hardcover)
ISBN: 1-880410-25-7 (CD-ROM)

The Certified Associate in Project Management (CAPM™) Role Delineation Study

Project Management Institute

This helpful book can answer many of your CAPM™ questions—and more! As project management grows in scope, importance and recognition, so do the related career options. Here, straight from the Project Management Institute (PMI®) is a look is a look at the latest important global certification. The CAPM certification lends professional credibility to men and women as they start their project management career path. This work tells the story of the development of the CAPM examination and outlines the knowledge a practitioner must master in order to pass the examination. Further, it offers a glimpse into the activities and responsibilities of CAPMs in the workplace. The Certified Associate in Project Management (CAPM) Role Delineation Study should be required reading for anyone who wants to pursue this certification.

ISBN: 1-880410-98-2 (spiral paperback)

Project Manager Competency Development Framework

Project Management Institute

Sharpen your project manager skills now! Discover the career benefits of climbing into the Project Management Institute's (PMI®) new competency development framework. Like an evolving building's transparent superstructure, the competency framework enables you to clearly see the interdependencies between your job knowledge, skills and behavior. Readily uncover areas of outmoded or faulty construction and tackle only what needs renovating. Enjoy the clarity! Researched by senior-level PMI members for four years, the Project Manager Competency Development Framework has the primary purpose of sharpening the skills of project management practitioners everywhere. It also guides the professional development of aspiring project management practitioners. Organizations will find the framework useful in guiding practitioners to their fullest potential. Individuals will find the framework useful in guiding the development of their own project management competence against a recognized standard.

ISBN: 1-880410-97-4 (paperback)

Proceedings of PMI Research Conference 2002

Project Management Institute

The Project Management Institute (PMI®) Research Conference 2002, Frontiers of Project Management Research and Application, co-chaired by Dennis P. Slevin, Ph.D., Jeffrey K. Pinto, Ph.D., and David I. Cleland, Ph.D., held 14-17 July in Seattle, Washington USA, brought together top researchers and practitioners in the project management field. Their purpose was to discuss new learning, ideas and practices, as well as answer questions in areas that may still need more work. This publication brings their research to your fingertips. The evolution of any profession depends on the breadth and depth of its research. The baselines must be established and then tested. Ideas must

grow and change to remain up-to-date with current issues and business practices in the world.
ISBN: 1-880410-99-0 (paperback)

Project Management Institute Practice Standard for Work Breakdown Structures

Project Management Institute

PMI's first practice standard to complement and elaborate on *A Guide to the Project Management Body of Knowledge (PMBOK® Guide) – 2000 Edition*, this new manual provides guidance and universal principles for the initial generation, subsequent development, and application of the Work Breakdown Structure (WBS). It introduces the WBS and its characteristics, discusses the benefits of using a WBS, and demonstrates how to build a WBS and determine its sufficiency for subsequent planning and control. A unique feature is the inclusion of 11 industry-specific examples that illustrate how to build a WBS, ranging from Process Improvement and Software Design to Refinery Turnaround and Service Industry Outsourcing.
ISBN: 1-880410-81-8 (paperback)

The PMI Project Management Fact Book, Second Edition

Project Management Institute

First published in 1999, this newly enlarged and updated "almanac" provides a single, accessible reference volume on global project management and the Project Management Institute (PMI®). Topics include the history, size, explosive growth, and the future of the project management profession; parameters of the typical project; a statistical profile of the individuals working in project management based on recent, global research; the organizational settings in which project management activities take place; and valuable information about the world's largest professional association serving project management, the Project Management Institute. Appendices offer an additional wealth of information: lists of universities with degree programs in project management and PMI Registered Educational Providers; PMI's Ethical Standards; professional awards; a glossary; and an extensive bibliography. This is the central reference for those working in project management and a career guide for those interested in entering the profession.
ISBN: 1-880410-73-7 (paperback)

People in Projects

Project Management Institute

Project management is fortunate in possessing a rich and growing body of tools and metrics that aid in helping us to more effectively run our projects. However, that is just what they are: tools and metrics. Project management is no less prone than any other discipline to the problems inherent in managing people. *In fact, a strong argument could be made that project management offers far more people problems than other forms of corporate activity* because it can involve so many levels of tasks, deadlines, cost pressures, the need to accomplish work through teams, and the well-known challenge of helping employees who have great technical skills also develop their people skills. This important book, *People in Projects,* focuses on one of the nine knowledge areas of *A Guide to the Project Management Body of Knowledge (PMBOK® Guide) – 2000 Edition:* human resource management. It is a collection of some of the most important writing relating to the people side of project management that the Project Management Institute has produced in the last six years.
ISBN: 1-880410-72-9 (paperback)

Project Management Experience and Knowledge Self-Assessment Manual

Project Management Institute

Based on the *Project Management Professional (PMP®) Role Delineation Study*, this manual is designed to help individuals assess how proficiently they could complete a wide range of essential project management activities based on their current levels of knowledge and experience. Included are exercises and lists of suggested activities for readers to use in improving their performance in those areas they assessed as needing further training.
ISBN: 1-880410-24-9 (spiral paperback)

Project Management Professional (PMP) Role Delineation Study

Project Management Institute

In 1999, the Project Management Institute (PMI®) completed a role delineation study for the Project Management Professional (PMP®) Certification Examination. In addition to being used to establish the test specifications for the examination, the study describes the tasks (competencies) PMPs perform and the project management knowledge and skills PMPs use to complete each task. Each of the study's tasks is linked to a performance domain (e.g., planning the project). Each task has three components to it: what the task is, why the task is performed, and how the task is completed. The *Project Management Professional Role Delineation Study* is an excellent resource for educators, trainers, administrators, practitioners, and individuals interested in pursuing PMP certification.
ISBN: 1-880410-29-X (spiral paperback)

The Future of Project Management

Project Management Institute

Developed by the 1998 PMI® Research Program Team and the futurist consultant firm of Coates and Jarratt, Inc., this guide to the future describes one hundred national and global trends and their implications for project management, both as a recognized profession and as a general management tool. It covers everything from knowbots, nanotechnology, and disintermediation to changing demography, information technology, social values, design, and markets.
ISBN: 1-880410-71-0 (paperback)

For additional PMI titles, please visit and shop our Online Bookstore at **www.pmibookstore.org**

Book Ordering Information

Phone: +412.741.6206
Fax: +412.741.0609
Email: pmiorders@abdintl.com
Mail: PMI Publications Fulfillment Center
               PO Box 1020
               Sewickley, Pennsylvania 15143-1020 USA

Visit PMI's website at **www.pmi.org**